St. Thomas, Nevada

T0288320

Wilbur S. Shepperson Series in Nevada History

Aaron McArthur

ST. THOMAS

NEVADA

A History Uncovered

Foreword by Senator Harry Reid

UNIVERSITY OF NEVADA PRESS

Reno & Las Vegas

Wilbur S. Shepperson Series in Nevada History
Series Editor: Michael S. Green

University of Nevada Press, Reno, Nevada 89557 USA
www.unpress.nevada.edu
Copyright © 2013 by University of Nevada Press
All rights reserved
Manufactured in the United States of
Design by Kathleen Szawiola

Library of Congress Cataloging-in-Publication Data

McArthur, Aaron.
 St. Thomas, Nevada : a history uncovered / Aaron McArthur.
 pages cm. — (Wilbur S. Shepperson series in Nevada history)
 Includes bibliographical references.
 ISBN 978-0-87417-919-4 (pbk. : alk. paper) — ISBN 978-0-87417-920-0 (e-book)
 1. Saint Thomas (Nev.)—History. I. Title. II. Title: Saint Thomas, Nevada.
 F849.S35M43 2013
 979.3'13—dc23   2013010402

Contents

Illustrations

Figures (following page 76)

Tables

Foreword

SENATOR HARRY REID

To some, the story of St. Thomas is a cautionary tale about water in the Southwest—or, rather, the lack of water. The followers of the Church of Jesus Christ of Latter-day Saints (LDS) who settled at the confluence of the Virgin and Muddy Rivers in 1865 knew a thing or two about the importance of water. After traveling for weeks in wagons across an unforgiving desert, that trickle of water, flowing constant in summer and winter, must have looked like a mirage.

And so they built a life there. It was a hard life, by all accounts. There was no air-conditioning and little shade from the scorching summers of southern Nevada. Walking from cistern to cistern in the ruins of St. Thomas, it is evident water made life there possible. But water—too much water—also put an end to St. Thomas.

The town never had more than a few hundred residents, even before construction began on the Hoover Dam, originally named the Boulder Dam, in 1931. A massive team of Depression-era engineers and builders set out to construct a forty-eight-million-dollar hydroelectric dam and massive reservoir to tame the mighty Colorado River and distribute its life-giving waters throughout the Southwest. The reservoir—Lake Mead—would extend more than one hundred miles back from the great dam and wipe St. Thomas off the map.

The Gentry Hotel, with its curved facade and second-story balcony, would soon be underwater. So would the schoolhouse, the rows of cottonwoods the settlers planted for shade, and the car repair shop where bachelors would crowd around the town's first radio to listen to the news. A few residents refused to leave until the waters were lapping at their doorsteps. In the end, however, they all moved on.

The town would rise again, though. When a mighty drought began early in the twenty-first century, the bones of St. Thomas peeked out from below the water. Concrete foundations, tree stumps, and the steps of the old schoolhouse emerged. In fact, a ghost town that had once been seventy feet below the middle of a lake was now a mile or more from the water's edge.

Some called the reemergence in 2002 a reminder of the harsh character of the desert, of the delicate balance of nature that makes life possible in inhospitable lands. After all, the residents of St. Thomas were not the first to abandon the valley. Nearly a thousand years ago, the Anasazi tribe left after living there for more than a thousand years. Their population had grown too quickly, and the land could no longer support them. The history of St. Thomas holds lessons about sustainability, stewardship of the land, and the value of water in the desert. St. Thomas has more to teach us as well.

The town also emerged from beneath the water once in the 1950s and again in the mid-1960s. In those days, there were reunions among the bones of buildings. Men and women who were only children when the lake took their homes gathered again to recall the faith that brought their parents and grandparents to the desert in the first place. They recalled the community they had built despite the harsh weather and the history they shared despite the town's short life span. The lessons they took from the loss of St. Thomas—and from its reemergence—were not about water. They were about community.

When St. Thomas emerged in 2002, however, there was no one left to remember that community. Almost everyone who ever lived in St. Thomas is dead. There will not be any more reunions. And that is a different kind of cautionary tale.

When I wrote my history of Searchlight, Nevada—the tiny hard-rock mining town where I grew up—I did twenty interviews or more with elderly residents, gathering stories from the early days of the last century. By the time I finished the book, seven of them were dead. It is a simple reality that eventually, no matter how long you live, you will lose your history if you do not write it down.

St. Thomas was an LDS community, and LDS are unusually good at writing down history. The records of St. Thomas are therefore relatively detailed.

Searchlight, on the other hand, had thirteen brothels but not a single church. We did not have the kind of record keeping there that will keep St. Thomas alive for generations to come, even though it has been gone for generations already.

Still, St. Thomas is a reminder that history is fleeting. The primary sources—our parents and their parents—will not be around forever. So we must be good stewards of their stories, preserving and conserving them as we do the natural resources that make life possible in the desert.

Preface

~~~~~~~~~~~~~~~~~

This book began as an administrative history of the St. Thomas, Nevada, site for the National Park Service. When the ruins of the town began to emerge from the murky depths of Lake Mead in 1999, the National Park Service realized that it needed to know how to administer the site. A few years later, I was recruited to write this administrative history by the late Hal Rothman, professor of history at the University of Nevada, Las Vegas. During the writing, I realized that the site had much to teach about western water issues and western history in general. It is this larger story of St. Thomas that I have expanded into this book.

There are many people who have helped in innumerable ways to bring this book to fruition. The staff at the LDS Archives, National Archives and Records Administration (NARA) in Denver, L. Tom Perry Special Collections at Brigham Young University, and Lied Library Special Collections at the University of Nevada, Las Vegas, went out of their ways to assist in my research. Though I spent less time at these institutions, I also found great help at the Denver Public Library, the Nevada State Museum, the Clark County Museum, Dixie State College, and the Boulder City Museum. Thanks are due to Virginia "Beezy" Tobiasson, who helped with some very good research leads.

I will be eternally grateful to Hal Rothman. He introduced me to David Louter, Steve Daron, and Rosie Pepito of the National Park Service, who were all wonderful resources during the research and writing phases and whose insights made this book better. Thanks are also due to Peter Michel for granting me time to work on the manuscript.

Thanks to my wife, Xela, and kids, Benjamin and Zion. Thank you for being patient with me during the time I spent writing and revising the manuscript. Sam, I haven't forgotten, SDG.

St. Thomas, Nevada

Introduction

In 2002, in the midst of the worst drought in recorded history in the Colorado River system, the remains of St. Thomas, onetime town on the Muddy River, emerged from the depths of Lake Mead. This mud-caked Brigadoon drew *Las Vegas Review-Journal* columnist John L. Smith for a visit. After pounding over the rutted road that wound through sandy washes and slogging over a mud flat to St. Thomas, Smith reveled in standing where pioneers once stood and in seeing what the Paiutes and Shoshones saw. While surveying the scene, he asked himself a question, "Why was lowly, mud-caked St. Thomas so important, and what can we still learn from it?" His answers focus on the fragility of life and the scarcity of water in the desert. St. Thomas, for Smith, exists to provide a cautionary tale about water, since Las Vegas's, and thus Nevada's, economic engine ultimately runs not on dice or cards, but on water. Smith's observations, though important, are mirrored by the scene he observed of the town emerging from the water. Much more lay hidden beneath the surface, waiting for time and determined searching to expose.[1]

Despite its lack of water, the southern Nevada region in which St. Thomas is located is full of history, recreation, defense industries, and cutting-edge architecture. The name Las Vegas, the biggest city in the area, carries a cachet that no other place in the world does. It is the entertainment capital of the world, a glittering jewel in the desert, a mecca for fun in the sun and in the Green Felt Jungle. The city has come to occupy a central position in popular American mythology. It is setting the pace for nationwide trends in city growth, demographics, immigration, consumption, work, and recreation. The history of that area then becomes important for understanding the society it birthed.[2]

One hundred and forty-five years ago, Las Vegas was a failed experiment. Missionaries from the Church of Jesus Christ of Latter-day Saints built a fort in the Las Vegas Valley in 1855, but poor relationships with the Southern Paiutes, crop failures, harsh weather, and the Utah War led to its abandonment in 1857. The political, economic, and social locus of the area was 60 miles to the east, in St. Thomas, Nevada. Located on the Muddy River, St. Thomas sat on the only significant water source for a 120-mile stretch of the Old Spanish Trail and became the main town on the Mormon supply line that stretched from the Colorado River to St. George, Utah. It was the first and most important town established in the Muddy Mission, the trailhead for mining expeditions and supply routes, and even a base of exploration for government surveys undertaken in preparation for the construction of a dam on the Colorado at Black Canyon. This book traces the history of the town, its importance in the region, its eventual demise, and its continuing significance in southern Nevada.

St. Thomas lies approximately 60 miles east of Las Vegas, Nevada, on the southern end of the Moapa Valley. Surrounded by great aridity, the town site benefited from its proximity to the spring-fed Muddy River and the Virgin River. The area has little rainfall, pervasive heat in the summer, frequent wind, and dust. Its official birth date was January 8, 1865, when Thomas Sassen Smith and his party of eleven men and three women arrived at the confluence of the Muddy and Virgin Rivers and founded the town. As an incorporated town, it ceased to exist in June 1938, when it went under the waters of Lake Mead. It is now part of the Lake Mead National Recreation Area.

Brigham Young established the town in part to secure Mormon self-sufficiency in the production of cotton. In January 1867, Congress took one degree of longitude from Utah Territory and gave it to Nevada. An accurate survey was not completed for nearly four years, during which time Nevada, Utah, and Arizona fought over who controlled much of what is now southern Nevada. As the primary settlement in the Muddy Mission of the Church of Jesus Christ of Latter-day Saints, St. Thomas played an important role in the conflict. The affair is a prime example of boundary conflicts between states. The town was the terminus of John Wesley Powell's 1869 expedition of the Grand Canyon. St. Thomas was a key water and rest stop on the Arrowhead Trail, the first all-weather road between Los Angeles and Salt Lake City. St. Thomas residents played a very important role in maintaining the road.

St. Thomas has national significance due to its relationship with the construction of the Hoover Dam, one of the most significant public works projects undertaken during the Great Depression. The town served as the base for survey crews; it illustrates some of the social issues of dam construction and provides the best publicly accessible previously inundated site from which to interpret dam construction. Other towns have, of course, been flooded by the construction of dams, but few are publicly accessible, let alone popular hiking destinations for area residents. It also remains significant for many Latter-day Saints whose ancestors lived in the town whose stories are occasionally told in conferences local and church-wide as well as in less formal settings.

In 1999 the site began to emerge from the murky depths, as it had on other occasions when drought conditions prevailed. Previous emergences triggered reunions of past residents and an outpouring of nostalgia for the time people spent there. St. Thomas seemed to belong solely to those who made their homes next to the Muddy River and their descendants. With the most recent emergence, however, National Park Service officials who administer the site and concerned citizens at large became interested in the secrets the former town has to share. The Park Service needed to know how to administer the site, and that need was the genesis for this book.

A study of St. Thomas can be taken as a microcosm of the study of the history of the US West. The more traditional view is informed by Frederick Jackson Turner's 1893 paper "The Significance of the Frontier in American History." Turner, and his later adherents, such as Roy Allen Billington, viewed the West as a process. The history of St. Thomas can certainly be fitted into a Turnerian mold. Spanish missionaries and explorers traveled through the area, which was inhabited by Native Americans, a people who Tunerians held were cunning, but devoid of "civilization." Miners attracted to the Pahranagat, Gold Butte, and Pioche mining strikes crossed and recrossed the countryside. Farmers moved in and established permanent settlements. The miners and farmers brought with them the eastern institutions of democracy in the form of mining districts as well as local, county, territorial, and state governments.

St. Thomas personifies all these processes and more. For a time, it operated as a quintessentially western community, full of wide-open violence, gambling, and speculation on mining claims as well as agricultural land. Residents went through the process of courting and obtaining railroad access, bringing with it fuller integration into the larger regional economy. The early history of the town can be taken as one where our pioneer ancestors took on the conditions and Indians and forged anew the democratic elements of American society.

The story of the town can also be presented as a vindication of the views expressed by "New Western" historians, most notably Patricia Limerick, Richard White, and Donald Worster. They reject Turner's "West as a process" thesis and have replaced it with "West as a place." They tend to focus on race, class, gender, and, to a lesser extent, the environment as prime movers in western history. Their view provides a useful framework for looking at the history of southern Nevada. In this New Western formulation, St. Thomas was not an outpost of white Anglo-Saxon Protestant culture on the frontier. Rather, it was a place where Mormons, Paiutes, miners, and Gentiles interacted in interesting ways. Excepting a few acres in the upper Muddy River valley, there was no reservation for the Southern Paiutes. Once the Mormons and miners had monopolized the best land and water in the area, there was nowhere to go, driving the Paiutes to wage labor or starvation. A discussion of the history of St. Thomas also needs to discuss gender, particularly because of the movement of polygamous wives through the town. It was outside of the territory of Utah, and therefore outside of the reach of federal marshals whose authority stopped at that territorial border.

This book also addresses religious motivations for settlement, as well as religious discrimination, as the government purchased land for the reservoir created by the Hoover Dam. As noted by Ferenc Morton Szasz in *Religion in the Modern American West,* too many scholars of the West ignore religion as a motivating factor in settlement. The settling of St. Thomas and the rest of the Muddy Mission gives us a clearer picture of the process Brigham Young went through when directing the settlement of a new area. Young is often characterized as a master colonizer, controlling every element of the process. It is true that when he sent people to create a new town, he tried to leave little to chance, making sure that the right people with the right skills were called to make the settlement viable. The story of St. Thomas shows that this was not always the case. Young did that only for certain communities—anchor communities, if you will—and let subsequent independent settlement fill in the nearby areas.

In *The American West Transformed: The Impact of the Second World War,* Gerald Nash discusses the far-reaching social, economic, and cultural changes that World War II brought to the West. The war certainly impacted southern Nevada, bringing Basic Magnesium, the Las Vegas Army Airfield (now Nellis Air Force Base), and eventually the Nellis and Tonopah bombing ranges. Well before the creation of the Nevada Test Site as a "national sacrifice area," another area was sacrificed for the needs of the country. This history of St. Thomas discusses the building of the Hoover Dam from the perspective of those who lived in the area inundated by the creation of the reservoir. It is unique in describing the survey and appraisal process that the federal government went through to acquire the land from its owners. It shows that the federal government had significant impacts on parts of the West well before the war.

Because the remains of St. Thomas lie within the boundaries of the Lake Mead National Recreation Area, which is a unit of the National Park Service, we are left with questions that are best addressed by the field of public history. The Park Service requires that any interested parties be given the opportunity to contribute to how park-owned resources are interpreted in their community. This means that although the town was founded by Mormons and inhabited almost solely by Mormons during its seventy-three-year life span, other stories are also important to tell. The history of the town belongs to the Paiutes, railroad workers, tourists, and government workers as well, and this book makes many of those stories known, as the final chapter discusses how the legacy of the town has changed since it went under water.

Finally, St. Thomas lies squarely in the midst of debates about water usage and its environmental impact on southern Nevada. Stories about the town figure into several recent articles about the region's growing water problem.

Clearly, the answer to John L. Smith's question "Why was lowly, mud-caked St. Thomas so important, and what can we still learn from it?" is much longer and more complex than can be answered in a newspaper editorial. We can learn about Native American history, Mormon history, western settlement, railroad expansion, community development, large-scale government projects, and the environment and discuss questions of remembrance and public memory. The mud-caked ruin that every so often tantalizingly rises from the waters of Lake Mead does indeed have much lying under the surface.

1

Physical Setting, Native American Usage, and Pre-Muddy Mission Mormon Movement

In 1864 the Samuel Claridge family lived in Nephi, Utah. Dressed in their finest clothes, they were eager to attend a meeting with the visiting president of the church, Brigham Young. Samuel's daughter Elizabeth described the meeting:

> During the afternoon we all attended the meeting, the girls in white having reserved seats in front. The sermons were inspirational and grand. They made us very happy until well on toward the close of the meeting when President Young announced that he had a few names to read—names of men who had been selected to go with their families and "settle the Muddy." That almost stopped our beating hearts. Many of our people had been previously called to settle the Dixie county. But the Muddy—that was so much farther—so much more difficult. Then I heard the name of Samuel Claridge, my father. After that I knew nothing for a moment and when I recovered myself again I was weeping bitterly. Tears were spoiling my new white dress but I sobbed on just the same. Said the companion who was at my side, "What are you feeling so badly about? My father has been called, too, but you see that I am not crying because I know he won't go." "That is just the difference. My father is called and I know that he WILL GO; and that nothing can prevent him from going. He never fails to do anything when called upon; and badly as I feel about it, I would be ashamed if he didn't go. But I will have no occasion to be ashamed for I tell you my father WILL GO."

Samuel Claridge did go to the Muddy, despite some initial problems. Just as the family was ready to depart, one of his horses was poisoned, and he had to buy another animal. A week later, one of his mules choked to death in the barn. Elizabeth related that some of their friends said, "Brother Claridge, this shows that you are not to go!" "Does it?" Elizabeth recalled her father saying. "It shows me," he continued, "that the adversary is trying to prevent me from going; but I am going all the same if I have to walk every foot of the way."[1]

The young Miss Claridge had some very concrete reasons for her consternation. Although not everyone who went to the Muddy had such a hard time getting there, all had the geography and climate to deal with, both of which could be very harsh. Explorers and settlers of European descent also encountered the Southern Paiutes who lived in the area. Sometimes they were very welcoming to newcomers, and other times they evinced serious hostility. Early interactions influenced both the positive and the negative relationships that the Mormons and Southern Paiutes had in the region. To understand the story of St. Thomas, we need to look at these things that so disconcerted Elizabeth and how they factored into general Mormon settlement motivations.

The Moapa Valley resembles much of the southern Great Basin, with steep, high mountains around relatively flat plains. The area is desert, averaging less than six inches of rain a year. Winter is mild, but the summer heat can be oppressive, with temperatures reaching up to 122 degrees. The valley's greatest asset is the spring-fed Muddy River. It is more of a stream than a river, but most important for the Paiutes and the Mormons who followed after, it flows year-round. The water and the area's lower elevation allowed for a longer growing season than St. George, which made the area desirable for cotton production. It was also the only water for fifty miles in every direction but south. There was plenty of grass for travelers' animals, which allowed for extended stays. Most journals of early travelers in the area mention the Muddy. Addison Pratt, one of the members of Jefferson Hunt's 1849 expedition through the area, said the water in the Muddy was warm and pleasant to bathe in. He also noted that the fish in the stream, which he thought resembled carp, were easy to catch. He also noted that the Paiutes' crops seemed to be doing well.[2]

Despite the presence of water, some travelers had very little positive to say about the Muddy. Parley P. Pratt wrote that the area was a "wide expanse of chaotic matter . . . lying in inconceivable confusion . . . a country in ruins, dissolved by the peltings of the storms of ages, or turned inside out, up side down, by terrible convulsions in some former age. . . . Poor and worthless."[3] Another traveler agreed with Pratt's estimation. He asked, "Was this Hades, Sheole, or the place for the condign punishment of the wicked, or was it the grand sewer for the waste and filth of vast animation?"[4]

Despite the low estimation that many whites had for the land, the Paiutes and their predecessors held the land in great regard, having inhabited the area for a millennium. The Paiutes believed their god Tabuts placed them on the land, and that act of placement made the land sacred.[5] The Paiutes were not the first Native American group to make the area that became St. Thomas their home. In 1931 near the Colorado River, archaeologists discovered the bones of an ancient sloth in a cave over the remains of human presence—charcoal, flint, and bones. The bones of the sloth were approximately twenty thousand years old.[6] The surrounding area contained evidence of human habitation eight thousand years ago.

Pueblo Grande de Nevada, also known as the Lost City, was the residence of a group of pueblo-dwelling Indians who lived in the area from about AD 100 to 1150. Lost City residents grew corn, beans, squash, gourds, and cotton; gathered seeds, turquoise, and paint materials; and hunted. Archaeological exploration showed that they had large trade networks from the shells found in the ruins. Given the evidence of extensive primitive salt mining, it is likely that salt was one of their main trade items. Hopi oral traditions suggest they are descended from people who lived on the Muddy. Some posit that drought, a stronger enemy, malaria, or yellow fever drove them from the area.[7]

By the time Europeans found their way to the Moapa Valley, the Southern Paiutes had long made it their home. They found the land along the Muddy very amenable to their lifestyle. In addition to water, the valley had other valuable resources. The Muddy had groves of the desert fan palm, which the Paiutes used for weaving baskets and bags and for the construction of shelters. The area that became St. Thomas was very well suited to their agriculture, being generally level and close to the confluence of the Muddy and the Virgin Rivers, which provided irrigation water. Parley P. Pratt noted in his 1852 visit to the area that the Paiutes were engaged in agriculture. He wrote that "sixty Muddy Indians in a state of nudity thronged the camp, bringing with them green corn, melons, and dressed skins in exchange for clothing." Addison Pratt noted that there were "fine fields of wheat, corn and beans, above us that belonged to the Indians." They "irrigated their lands from this stream and their field had the appearance of bearing a very heavy crop."[8] In the June 19, 1868, issue of the *Deseret News*, Joseph W. Young also reported on their farming practices. He said they planted their wheat in hills, one to two feet apart, and watered it often, but did not let the water stand and soak. He said this created large heads and full berries, so much so that he "never saw finer grain in [his] life." The Paiutes also gathered wild plants to supplement their diet. They mixed mesquite meal with water and made it into huge cone-shaped loaves. These loaves weighed as much as fifty pounds. The Paiutes would then dry them for winter storage.

Whites who did not understand the exigencies of surviving in the desert with limited technology derided the Paiutes' eating habits. The Southern Paiutes were also referred to as "Diggers" by whites due to their habit of carrying a stick with which they constantly probed and dug, looking for edible roots, insects, and reptiles. For the less gastronomically adventurous whites, the Paiutes seemed to have no compulsion against eating absolutely anything they could get their hands on. One early visitor observed, "They ate lizards, snakes, grasshoppers, locusts and crickets, ants, and even the vermin which infested their furry clothing and their own hair." Another visitor presented the Paiutes on the Muddy with some dried beef that had gotten wet and was spoiled and moldy. As disgusting as the beef was to the white man, the Paiutes ate it "voraciously." After consuming the beef and some coffee, they "expressed their satisfaction by rubbing down their stomachs, and grunting in a manner which would have done credit to a herd of well-fed swine."[9] No doubt, the eating habits of the white man seemed ridiculous or at least wasteful to the Paiutes as well.

Cultural differences between the Paiutes and early explorers led to further misunderstandings. The lack of clothing in Paiute living offended Christian sensibilities. Men generally wore a breechclout and women a skirt. For warmth, those possessing them wore robes. John C. Frémont was not kind in his estimation of the tribe. In his memoirs, he wrote, "In these Indians I was forcibly struck by an expression of countenance resembling that in a beast of prey; and all their actions are those of wild animals. Joined to the restless motion of the eye, there is a want of mind—and absence of thought—and an action wholly by impulse, strongly expressed and which strongly expressed the similarity." They followed Frémont's group "stealthily, like a band of wolves." Any livestock allowed to straggle was quickly stolen and eaten.[10] In all fairness, by stopping along the Muddy, Frémont's men had been feeding their animals on grasses that the Paiutes used for a large part of their diet.

Though Frémont attributed their cunning to that of wild animals, the Paiutes were very wise when it came to surviving in a harsh environment. Almost as invidious as the belief that they were savages was the notion that the Paiutes were "children of Nature" and lived simply and free of care. The Mormons who came later had somewhat softer prejudices against their Native American neighbors, but still held some of the notions evidenced in Frémont's account.

Running directly through the Muddy River valley, the St. Thomas area provided an important stop on the Old Spanish Trail. Mexicans, white Americans, and Native Americans used the trail extensively for exploration and traffic in fur, liquor, guns, horses, and Native American child slaves. Though beaver are scarce in southern Nevada today, various trappers sought them in the area in the early nineteenth century. Accounts are spotty in part because Mexican authorities made trapping on the Colorado or its tributaries illegal, so any activity had to be clandestine.[11]

Jedediah Strong Smith passed through the area in 1826. With 15 men, he went south from the Provo area, following a trail used by Father Escalante down the Sevier River. He then followed the Virgin past the Muddy and traveled across the Mojave to San Bernardino.[12] By the time the Saints arrived in the Great Basin, great caravans were traveling up and down the trail.[13] In 1842 a party of 194 New Mexicans on their way to trade in California stopped to rest on the Muddy with 4,150 cattle and horses. Every caravan that came through stopped at least overnight, and often for several days, as their animals grazed on the abundant grass in the valley.[14]

For travelers on the Old Spanish Trail, the importance of the water running down the Muddy may be hard to overstate. The next nearest accessible water was the Las Vegas Springs in one direction and springs in Utah in the other direction. In May 1844, Frémont left Las Vegas for the Muddy. His party had not traveled far when they came upon the skeletons of horses, mute testimony to the consequences of not finding water in the desert. As they traveled, the desert floor reflected the heat of the sun, baking them from the bottom as well as the top. Occasionally, they would chop into a *bisnaga*, a ferocactus, to get at the pulp, or chew on the leaves of sour dock to moisten their mouths. When the group had been marching for sixteen hours with the sun over the horizon for several hours, their mules suddenly began to run forward. After another two miles, the weary travelers reached the Muddy, which Frémont called the Rio de Los Angeles.[15] Though the water was greatly appreciated, Frémont called the Muddy the "most dreary river" he had ever seen.[16]

Attorney and future Oregon Supreme Court justice Orville C. Pratt recorded a more positive experience on the Muddy, although traveling in a different direction from Frémont. Upon reaching the river, his party "made a delightful camp on a fine stream of water with good grass." They had a pleasant meal of corn and beans purchased from the Paiutes while they looked around in appreciation. Pratt wrote, "The valley of 'Muddy' is large & land fertile. The water is of the best and purest kind and some day, & that not too distant, this valley will teem with a large & healthy population." The desirability of the Muddy River was highlighted by his observations on his subsequent march to Las Vegas. He wrote, "Our march was a very hard one of full 50 m. & one of the mules failed by the way side. Not a drip of water or a spear of grass the whole distance."[17]

When Kit Carson traveled through the area in 1844, he also had to contend with the Paiutes and the environment. While camping on the Muddy, Carson was approached by about three hundred Paiutes who wanted to come into his camp. He refused, telling them that they had killed seven Americans the year before and they were treacherous creatures who could not be trusted. He explained that he felt the only reason they wanted to enter his camp was to maintain the guise of friendship long enough to kill his party, and if they did not leave, he would open fire. One Paiute was killed when the group refused to leave, and then the others withdrew. Carson had no more trouble with them after that.[18]

One of the biggest reasons that Americans traveling through the area ran into conflicts with the Paiutes is that the Americans did not understand the importance of reciprocity to the Paiutes. When one Paiute band had a lean year, other bands provided food so that nobody starved, even if everyone was hungry. Another band could enter lands traditionally occupied by another if they did so to survive. If one Paiute band used the resources of another, they had to contribute what they could in return. The exigencies of living in such a tough environment required everyone to conform to this behavior. Livestock consumed and trampled huge amounts of grass that would normally provide seeds for Paiute winter supplies. Since the travelers would not contribute to the general welfare after they had consumed so many resources, the Paiutes felt justified in doing whatever they could to extract some food from the situation.[19]

Scholars disagree as to who named the river the Muddy River, whites or Native Americans, and, if whites, who named it first. Jedediah Smith (1826), Kit Carson (1847), and Orville Pratt (1848) all referred to the stream as the Muddy. In the *Deseret News*, Joseph W. Young claimed that the term *Muddy River* originated because the Old Spanish Trail crossed the valley near a low alkali swamp that proved hard to cross in wet weather. Young remembered the water as clear and good to drink but too warm for pleasant drinking. Historian James McClintock claimed to have seen a map of the New Mexico Territory from 1853 that called the stream El Rio Atascoso, denoting a miry place where the traffic sticks fast, rather than a river that is muddy its entire length.[20] Lieutenant Edward Beale, another explorer, referred to the Muddy by its Spanish name. Frémont was apparently the only one to call the stream Rio de Los Angeles.

Some sources suggest that the name Muddy is from a Paiute word for "mesquite." Their term for the mesquite bean is *moudy*, and many mesquite trees grow along the stream. Visitor Perry Liston offered a different explanation. When he visited the Muddy in 1857, he claimed that the Paiutes referred to the stream as *ma-pat*, which means "muddy water." The Muddy River may have obtained its moniker when whites adopted what the Paiutes already called it. Even if that is not the case, the name seems appropriate if both groups arrived at it individually. The source of the name of the Moapa Valley is much clearer. The Paiutes called the valley *Moa-pah*, meaning "water valley."[21]

Mormons established St. Thomas in 1865, but the Church of Jesus Christ of Latter-day Saints arrived in the area two decades prior. In 1847, the same year that the Saints reached the valley of the Great Salt Lake, Jefferson Hunt, having recently mustered out of the Mormon Battalion, led a party from Salt Lake to Los Angeles. The church sent him to buy seeds and explore the area between Salt Lake and the ocean. Hunt followed the Old Spanish Trail. The next year Howard Egan, under the direction of Brigham Young, carefully surveyed every possible campsite between Provo and Southern California, noting the natural resources available at each possible stop. The church utilized this information to publish a guide for travelers.[22]

On his way to the mission field, LDS apostle Parley P. Pratt stopped briefly on the Muddy. He noted that although getting there was a challenge, the valley was well watered, had good soil and fuel, and had sufficient grass to support a settlement of one to two hundred families. Agriculture was feasible given that the Paiutes were already growing wheat and corn.[23] He also noted the area lacked timber for building. Since Pratt was an apostle, it is certain that this information made it back to LDS president Brigham Young. By 1854 records clearly show that President Young contemplated establishing a settlement near the Colorado River. Given the extremely mild winters, cotton, indigo, and other tropical plants and fruits would grow there. A southern settlement would also benefit those whose health suffered in Utah winters. He went so far as to tell church member John Eldridge that he was free to start such a settlement if he so desired.[24]

In the meantime, some Paiutes along the Muddy invited the Saints to settle in the area. Brigham Young believed the rest of the Moapa Paiutes would welcome LDS settlement. The southern Paiutes were much weaker militarily than the neighboring Ute and Navajo. The Paiutes feared the Ute in particular because they captured Paiute children and sold them into slavery in Mexico. The Paiutes hoped the Saints would serve as buffers between them and slave-raiding parties as well as become trade partners. The Paiutes also wished to bring the Saints, with their greater resources, into their system of reciprocity.[25]

In response to their invitation, leaders of the Southern Indian Mission sent Rufus Allen to the Muddy to teach the Paiutes the "Restored Gospel." Allen's missionaries baptized 230 Paiutes on the Muddy in 1855.[26] Since the Paiutes in the valley were now members, church leaders no doubt felt they would continue to welcome Mormon settlements in the area. A letter that Brigham Young sent to George W. Armstrong, Indian agent, evidences this belief. Young wrote, "The natives . . . on the Rio Virgin and Muddy are very peaceful, and are extremely anxious to learn and adopt the manners and customs of civilized life. Good policy aside from more important considerations, dictates the encouragement of that feeling, and the furnishing of the proper facilities therefor."[27]

Perhaps the most interesting settlement proposed for the Muddy was one for Sandwich, or Hawaiian, islanders who had joined the church and desired to be "gathered to Zion," since they were unable to find a suitable gathering place on the archipelago. President Young felt it unwise to have the islanders settle with the Saints at San Bernardino or nearby where they could be "contaminated" by "Gentile" Californian settlers.[28] Young said the soil was good and the climate was much more similar to that of their native land than areas farther north. On the Muddy, they would have "every reasonable facility for applying all the skill & industry they are at present possessed of, & above all, they will be in the midst of a mild spirited, industrious portion of the remnants of Jacob, their blood brethren, who are welcoming our missionaries with warm hearts & open arms."[29]

The "warm hearts & open arms" did not last long. William Bringhurst, the leader of the Saints at Las Vegas, explored the entire Muddy Valley in early 1856. Bringhurst reported that the valley was "probably a better place to colonize" than Las Vegas was. He found that many of the Moapa Paiutes were sick and had become very suspicious of the whites. Evidently, a band of Ute told them that the white men were going to take all their land.[30] Despite the Paiutes' less than cordial welcome, Bringhurst's appraisal of the valley reached Brigham Young.

In September 1856, President Young wrote to Bringhurst, advising him to remain in the Las Vegas settlement. However, Young did give his permission for all not actively engaged in producing lead to establish a settlement on the Muddy. Brigham reasoned that the Muddy offered "a good opening for extensive farms suitable for cotton growing," which the church could use to clothe the Saints, lessening their dependence on cloth brought in from the East. Despite this encouragement, President Young made it very clear that settlement on the Muddy should take place only if there were truly too many people in Las Vegas, since the standing excuse of those in that mission was that there was insufficient work for all there.[31] President Young also discussed the possibility of cotton production on the Muddy with Miles Anderson, another Las Vegas Saint.[32]

One of the main reasons the church continued to establish new settlements on the periphery of lands controlled by the Saints was to provide as much buffer as possible between the main body of the Saints and the "Gentiles," or nonmembers, with whom the church had experienced poor relationships since the establishment of the church in 1830. The Saints had been driven out of Ohio, Missouri, and Illinois by their non-LDS neighbors, and their founder, Joseph Smith, had been killed by a mob. Church leadership had no desire to have similar events happen again in the Great Basin.

In 1857 a group of Saints happened upon Lieutenant Joseph C. Ives of the Corps of Topographical Engineers who was exploring the Colorado River under the orders of the secretary of war. When President Young found out

about the expedition, he sent George A. Smith to explore the area and identify places for settlement to preempt the arrival of any non-Mormon settlers.[33] Activities like this were not limited to what is now southern Nevada.
Young was intent on securing all the lands claimed by the Mormons in the
proposed state of Deseret and sent explorers and settlers throughout the
Great Basin and surrounding areas, eventually establishing more than five
hundred settlements throughout the West.[34]

In addition to worrying about Gentile settlement, 1857 also saw the deterioration of the relationship with the Paiutes. Historian of the Southern
Utah Mission James G. Bleak recorded that on his way to Las Vegas from
the St. George area, he learned of Paiute plans to attack his party while they
camped. The Paiutes believed they could easily kill the men and obtain a
large amount of spoil. Once the party arrived at the Muddy, Bleak called the
Paiutes together. They sat and smoked some tobacco that Bleak had brought
for that purpose. He told them, "You have listened to my talk in times past,
you believe that it is good to hear, and do what I say," to which the Paiutes
agreed. Bleak told them that they were going to California with some friends
to trade the goods that they had brought. He expressed his desire that if any
animals were to stray, they would be returned. Some of the Paiutes did not
readily consent to let the company pass in peace.

To secure a peaceful resolution, Bleak asked the Paiutes to send for their
women and children whom they had sent into hiding, as was the custom
of the Paiutes whenever strangers were around. Bleak then spent the evening and most of the night with them so they could not make a large-scale
move without his knowledge. The next day, Bleak's party continued on to
Las Vegas. The plan of the Paiutes on the Muddy had apparently been long
in the making, because while at Las Vegas, residents informed Bleak that
news of the proposed attack had reached the fort there. As the group continued on to California, three Native Americans who attempted to steal from
them followed Bleak's party. The Mormons captured the Native Americans,
kept them overnight, and released them the next morning. The party had no
more problems with Native Americans for the rest of the trip.[35]

To try to improve their relationship with the Paiutes and keep travelers going between San Bernardino and Utah safe, church leaders sent Jacob
Hamblin and Ira Hatch to spend some time on the Muddy. Hatch arrived in
January 1858. His record indicates he lived there alone "among the savages"
for at least two weeks. Since the Saints abandoned the Las Vegas mission in

1857, the nearest white settlement was Fort Clara, a one-hundred-mile trip. Hatch camped in a broken-down wagon left on the side of the road and had considerable difficulty keeping his food in his own possession. Generally cooking in the evening, Hatch waited until the Paiutes had retired to their own camp before he pulled his food out of wherever he had it concealed. They finally discovered where he kept his food. While Hatch interpreted for some travelers, some Paiutes stole his bread and meat, leaving him only a little cheese. To console him, they told Hatch he should not feel bad, because he could beg travelers for food and they would give it to him because he was white.[36] Both Hatch's and Hamblin's missions were successes, at least enough that Bleak's *Annals* does not tell of any incidents along the Muddy for the duration of their time there.

Up until 1858, discussions of cotton growing at the Southern Utah Mission, also known as Utah's Dixie, were strictly speculative. In order to test the feasibility of producing cotton, Brigham Young sent a group of sixteen men who were experienced in growing cotton to Santa Clara to experiment.[37] Many Saints viewed a call to move to the Southern Utah Mission tantamount to exile. Church leaders very carefully emphasized that this was not the case. Speaking to a group of cotton missionaries in 1862, Heber C. Kimball said, "God is inspiring this mission, and only those should go who can be relied upon, for the leaders [have] been careful to select good men. No man [was] called with the thought of getting rid of him."[38] As was the pattern when settling any other LDS community, Young and other leaders were careful to select people not only for their faith and willingness to go when called, but also so that all important trades were represented, such as blacksmiths, coopers, wheelwrights, carpenters, and so on.

LDS efforts to establish a town on the Muddy finally passed beyond a mere proposal and began to take shape in 1864. There were several reasons behind establishing St. Thomas on the Muddy, though most sources generally cite only one—cotton production. There is no doubt that cotton was a motivating factor for church leadership in establishing St. Thomas. The Civil War interrupted Southern cotton production, and freighting material in from the East was already expensive. Brigham Young wanted to promote cotton production to help the Utah Saints become more self-sufficient.

Another reason scholars mention as a motivation to settle on the Muddy was to take up all available lands before the Gentiles had an opportunity to do so. Having been driven out of Ohio, Missouri, and Illinois by their non-Mormon neighbors, the Saints were not heartened by the prospect of a non-Mormon population developing in their new home. Closely related to this concern is that President Young was also adverse to the Saints' getting involved with precious-metal mining, saying that the love of money distracted the faithful from focusing on what was important. At a meeting in Panaca in 1865, Erastus Snow reinforced that policy, stating the church would excommunicate any man who left their community for the mines.[39] President Young recognized significant mining opportunities in Mormon-controlled territory and knew if the Saints did not lay claim to them, Gentiles certainly would. Because of that, the First Presidency sent people to actively locate and claim all valuable mining areas in what is now southern Nevada. Church leaders claimed silver deposits in Meadow Valley, claims that would eventually pass to Gentiles and form the basis of the rush that created Pioche, Nevada.

Ira Hatch was one of the men sent by the church to locate claims. Hatch was a loyal member of the church who would not have violated the injunction against mining unless directly instructed by his leaders. His party located claims in the Pahranagat Valley and established a mining district. Usually, when miners established districts, they were not very creative in writing the rules—they simply copied the laws from other districts and got down to the business of mining. Hatch's group departed from this tradition and established rules specifically designed to suppress any general rush to the area. Their laws allowed them to monopolize the best properties, permanently hold title to their claims, and deny future claims. They did this while letting their own properties remain undeveloped.[40] The Saints were unsuccessful in keeping out the Gentiles, and the boom in the Pahranagat spawned Hiko, the eventual seat of Lincoln County.

Beyond simply keeping Gentiles out of the area, President Young recognized that the church needed to occupy the land. In early January 1865, before the missionaries sent to the Muddy had even arrived, Young sent a letter to all the bishops and general authorities in the church to promote settlement in that area. He wrote:

> [The] reports which we have received from the southern part of our Territory . . . to the Colorado River are of so favorable a character that we are desirous that a number of families should go down there as early as practicable and make settlements and secure the land. The knowledge of the advantages which settlements

there offers [sic] is not much known outside of our Territory at present; but, when it becomes known that we are making efforts to open a door for our trade to come in by that way, the news will soon spread, and we may reasonably expect that parties who have an eye to money-making will seek to take possession and profit by our labors, unless we by prompt action, forestall them. If there are any well-disposed, faithful brethren, who have families in your settlements who have a desire to move on to the Colorado, or in that vicinity, we would be pleased to have you inform us as soon as you can, and we will give you further instructions as to what they should do.[41]

When present, the men did a good job of holding off Gentile incursions; however, simply sending men like Ira Hatch to camp out for a few weeks at a time was not sufficient to permanently hold the land. Entire families needed to settle to accomplish that aim. Despite the Mormon presence in the wider area, it was not until March 1864 that the First Presidency called George Brimhall to explore the viability of settlement near the Colorado River. In order to get an accurate feel for what the trip would really be like for families called to settle there, Brimhall took his family with him.[42]

In addition to George Brimhall, President Young sent others in preparation of a settlement effort on the Muddy. In February 1864, Young instructed Jacob Hamblin to locate the best route for a road from St. George to the mouth of the Virgin River on the Colorado. Young said that he considered erecting a telegraph line and wanted to place it along the most traveled route. According to historian Melvin T. Smith, the church also contemplated a railroad line from St. George to the Colorado as early as 1864, an idea repeated for various routes in 1868 and 1881.[43]

Scholars have posited several other reasons for the establishment of St. Thomas and the Muddy Mission. In 2007 apostle Jeffrey R. Holland proposed that the Saints felt obligated to work with the Paiutes. Others claim that President Young expressed concern that other Christian denominations had sent missionaries to Utah to bring Mormons back to a more traditional Christianity. These theorists believe Young worried that the Saints were getting soft and might wander from the path if not toughened up by some sacrifice. James H. Wood, a modern-day descendant of Muddy missionary William Wood, wrote that church leadership sent William to the Muddy because he "was showing signs of progress that were too rapid, affluence that was too competitive for the Authorities to accept without question." President Young did say, however, that one of the reasons for settling southern Utah was to provide hiding places for those who would love and serve God.[44]

The last main reason Brigham Young initiated settlement on the Muddy was to aid in the movement of goods and people from the Colorado River into Utah. Shipping goods overland was very expensive, so President Young wanted to build a shipping depot at the head of navigation on the Colorado and ship goods from the East around South America and up the Colorado River. He also contemplated sending all people emigrating to Utah from across the Atlantic over the Isthmus of Panama and up the river, which would be a much easier walk than two-thirds of the way across the United States. At a meeting in Salt Lake City on November 11, 1864, Anson Call received a calling to build a warehouse on the Colorado to receive goods.[45] Settlements on the route to St. George "for resting places and as supports and strength for the warehouse and road" were to be established. Planners sold sixteen thousand dollars in stock to the public to fund the venture. President Young felt the route was necessary for the shipping of goods and emigration and did not anticipate any serious difficulty in making the route "safe for every purpose for which we may need it."[46] Call and his companions left Salt Lake City on November 15, 1864, a mere week after President Young appointed them to their mission.

Call reported positive prospects for the warehouse and supporting settlements. He found a suitable spot on the Colorado River, relaying that the Colorado was about the size of the Illinois River and possessed a landing that was as good as the Peoria landing in Illinois. The flowers were in bloom, and he found a patch of ripening watermelons "growing thriftily." The areas he recommended for settlements were near the confluence of the Virgin and the Muddy and Beaver Dam. He estimated that it would cost sixty thousand dollars to make a good road to the new landing from St. George.[47] Call named the new settlement Callville.

Along with preparations for the construction of the warehouse, plans also went forward for settlements to support the river traffic. In the October 1864 General Conference of the church, leaders called thirty-five families to establish homes on the Muddy.[48] Brigham Young did not announce the names of those who would lead the settlements at the meeting, but on November 11, 1864, Thomas Sassen Smith and Henry W. Miller of Farmington received notice that they would bear that responsibility.[49]

People called to settle on the Muddy in the initial and subsequent calls had a variety of reactions when they heard the news. William Wood sold his butcher shop, slaughterhouse, and brick home that had cost him four thousand dollars. Within four weeks, he was ready to go.[50] Hannah Sharp received the news of her husband's call nine days after she gave birth to, and lost, her first child. The brethren came to her house while her husband was away. She fainted at the news. When she apprised her husband of the call, he wanted to go with some of the other families and come for her later. She refused that arrangement, so they traveled to the Muddy together.

For people living in a secular society, they may wonder why anyone so unhappy about a call would be willing to carry it out. The answer lies in the *Doctrine and Covenants,* a collection of what believers accept as revelations given to Joseph Smith and his successors as president of the church. Section 1, verse 38, reads: "What I the Lord have spoken, I have spoken, and I excuse not myself, and though the heavens and hearth pass away, my word shall not pass away, but shall all be fulfilled, *whether my mine own voice or by the voice of my servants, it is the same*" (emphasis added). A call to settle was not simply the whim of a church leader; the Saints believed it was the will of the Lord.

There was nothing new about the presence of people on the Muddy. Human habitation stretched back for millennia. The area was, however, about to enter a new phase in history. For the first time in the Muddy's recorded history, a group of people deliberately colonized the area. Their willingness to settle and stay in the harsh environment shows the resolve and obedience the people had to leaders they felt spoke for God. That resolve was tested repeatedly by harsh weather, the scarcity of resources, tensions with their Paiute neighbors, and everyday life in newly settled areas.

2

Establishing an Outpost of Zion

The January 18, 1865, edition of the *Deseret News* contained a report by Anson Call on a trip through the area on his way to El Dorado Canyon. He wrote:

Every facility seems to abound here to warrant the establishment of a large self-sustaining settlement. . . . Dec. 1st. This morning we crossed the river and passed up on the upper side of the Muddy. We were well pleased with the extent of land and with the quality. . . . The muddy is about the size of Big Cottonwood clear, and water of a good quality. . . . Most of the land is suitable for cultivation. . . . Convenient to the place, opportunity most suitable for settlement, is to be found large quantities of sand-stone. . . . [T]he road traveled today is naturally good, our guide talked with many of the Indians met by us today. They are anxious for us to settle the country, and are willing for our cattle to eat their grass, if we will employ them that they may have clothes to wear and food to eat when their grass seed is all used.

As if high-quality land, plenty of water, available building material, and friendly Native residents were not enough, Call mentioned the rock-salt quarry, with "thousands of tons" available for nothing more than the effort of extracting it. Punctuating his glowing report, Call wrote that on their return trip, they "more thoroughly examined the facilities for forming a settlement on the Muddy; our examinations proved highly satisfactory, exhibiting greater facilities than we at first anticipated." He neglected, however, to mention the man-, animal-, and equipment-punishing trip involved in getting there or the agonizingly brutal summer weather, let alone that the nearest timber for building would involve a drive that would be long even with a modern pickup.

Establishing a Mormon community involved much more than just finding a promising spot of land. Site selection, who would settle, and often when they would travel to the site were all determined by leaders in Salt Lake City. As previously discussed, Brigham Young decided to create a settlement on the Muddy River. The ecclesiastical domination continued with the establishment, surveying, and peopling of St. Thomas, all of which conformed to eighteen years of Mormon settlement patterns in Deseret. The missionaries often experienced great hardship reaching the Muddy River, and most notably the harsh desert conditions the summers brought once they were there. These missionaries encountered great difficulties in reaching the Muddy and creating a viable community once they arrived. This was in part due to the scarcity of trees and other preferred building materials that encouraged creativity in the construction of their dwellings.

St. Thomas residents were involved in many things that parallel larger American settlement patterns of the West: the telegraph, farming, irrigation, mining, simple entertainments, and more. Because the area they settled in was already inhabited, there were many cultural misunderstandings with their Native American neighbors, violence and reprisals on both sides, treaties, and the white utilization of Paiute labor. This chapter also discusses St. Thomas as the terminus for John Wesley Powell's initial exploration of the Grand Canyon.

It is vital to understand that the single most important organization in St. Thomas and the rest of the settlements in the Muddy Mission was the Church of Jesus Christ of Latter-day Saints. It could hardly be otherwise, since most of the residents would never have moved there, much less remained, but for their spiritual leaders directing them to go. Residents held meetings regularly, and the church building was the nicest building in town. They usually closely followed the wishes of the church and its leaders, which they believed to be the wishes of God. Though the Saints were experiencing difficulties with the state of Nevada, the Southern Paiutes, and the environment itself, the fate of the town would be decided by church leaders. Because their leaders asked them to be there, they were determined to make it work.

The town of St. Thomas was born on January 8, 1865, when Thomas S. Smith, eleven other men, and three women arrived at the Muddy. Geography determined the town's location. The eroded, waterless desert between the Muddy and St. George did not lend itself to wagon travel, so most travelers followed the Virgin River south. This route was also difficult because the Virgin generally meanders between steep and rocky embankments, making it necessary to ford the river more than thirty times, the exact number changing from season to season as it meanders in its floodplain. The Virgin meets the Muddy within sight of the location selected for St. Thomas. Brigham Young instructed that the town be established as close to the Colorado landing as possible. Smith chose the land closest to the river that could support a settlement. Others quickly joined Smith's party, swelling the group to forty-five families. A Gentile named Elias McGinnies joined this initial group of Mormons in St. Thomas and drew lots with the Saints when they distributed the land. Seemingly, Gentiles in Zion were not a problem if they were in small numbers—or else McGinnies had a particularly good relationship with the leaders of the settlement. A Paiute known as Old Bishop also accompanied the Saints. It is not clear from the records if he was a Mormon, though his name implies he was. Old Bishop watched their livestock at night while on the trail.[1]

Hannah Sharp's account of her trip to the Muddy shows some of the difficulties the missionaries faced simply getting to the new town. Sharp was terrified of water, yet their passage required crossing the Virgin River thirty-four times. After the first white-knuckle crossing of the river, she turned to her husband and said, "John, I'd rather you would hang me than take me through that water again." Nevertheless, she survived the subsequent crossings. Water was not the only factor that made the passage down the Virgin so treacherous. Wind blew sand across the road for miles. The sand would, as Sharp put it, "pour over the wheels like treacle from a jug." One crossing that she said was a block long combined water and quicksand, making it especially dangerous.[2] The Sharps made it through unscathed, but occasionally missionaries found themselves stalled out in the river. Trapped, they waited either to have their outfits swept away or for another team to pull them out of the muck.

Coming down the Virgin was not the only way to get to the valley, but by most accounts it was the easiest. William Wood came down through what is now central Nevada. The roads were so bad that he ended up leaving many of the items he brought, including a stove, at the side of the trail. At one point, he had to disassemble his wagon and lower it over a cliff to continue. Whatever the route, the difficulty took a physical toll on the travelers. George Lowe, an early resident, remembered the challenge of walking four hundred miles with his father to get to the Muddy.[3]

Such a walk may have been unpleasant, but it did avoid the precipitous entry into the valley from the mesa overlooking the river. Elizabeth Claridge's journal records the dangerous entry. The beginning of the nearly mile-long descent into the Moapa valley is almost perpendicular, which required the wagons to be triple-teamed and frequent blocking of the wheels to allow the horses to rest. In some places, the wagons had to be lowered by chains. Making Elizabeth's passage even more complicated was that the wind "blew a perfect hurricane." They seemed to make good progress until disaster stuck. She recorded:

> But lo! A crash! The tongue that was broken in the river gave way and down came the wagon; as the massive thing dashed past me, it drug my dress under the wheel. How narrow was my escape from being crushed to death! The wagon rolled down a ways then suddenly plunged over the side of the precipice. Now, it tumbled over and over scattering the flour and other provisions all over the hillside. I shall never forget the look of consternation on the faces of that group as they stood gazing at the destruction spread out below.[4]

Once the Saints made it safely to the valley, they commenced establishing their settlement. As they lacked legal title to the land, they occupied it by squatters' rights. They laid out the town with eighty-five one-acre town lots, eighty-five two-and-a-half-acre lots for vineyards, and the same number of five-acre farm lots. Ten town lots formed a block. According to Bleak's *Annals*, the streets were six rods wide and included twelve-foot sidewalks. The survey was not exact; settlers paced off the measurements. The methods used place St. Thomas squarely within the traditions of Mormon town founding.

Doctrine and Covenants 132:8 reads, "Behold, mine house is a house of order, saith the Lord God, and not a house of confusion," and Mormons laying out towns took that phrase to heart. The Mormon village is unique in the West, since most communities grew up more organically. Joseph Smith's plat for the city of Zion (1833) is not part of the Mormon scriptural canon. Nevertheless, Mormons followed it in spirit, if not in practice, all throughout the West. The plat was one mile square, and all the squares on the plat contained ten acres. The lots were laid with every other block facing north-south, the others east-west. A square for public buildings occupied the center. The plat reserved land away from the town lots for barns and stables. The plan also apportioned farmland.

Geographer Donald Meinig portrays the city of Zion as a rigid gridiron of roomy blocks and streets in which one is able to discern the influence of the plans of New England towns, but Mormon towns were formalized by the biblical foursquare and expressed a firm belief in the virtue of social concentration and of a rationally ordered society, which was a worthy setting for the Kingdom of God on earth. A city built on the plan, according to Smith, would be able to hold twenty thousand people. Distinct from New England towns, though, Smith added space at the center for monumental architecture, for the construction of twenty-four temples. These temples were more like civic structures than traditional meetinghouses. According to Wallace Stegner, the result was "a right-angled and rather stiff-elbowed version of the garden city, created well ahead of its time and demonstrating the advantages of an orderly town-building over the hit-and-miss squatting that characterized the usual western settlement."[5]

LDS Church founder Joseph Smith had reasons for the plat beyond a simple desire for order. In a letter accompanying the plat for the city of Zion, he enumerated the benefits accrued by settling in a nucleated pattern. Farmers and their families were often isolated from society by the distance they had to travel to population centers from their farms. However, society "has been, and always will be, the great educator of the human race." Improved access to village life meant all the advantages found in schools, public lectures, and other meetings. Blessing their homes would be the "same intellectual life, the same social refinement as will be found in the home of the merchant or banker or professional man." Brigham Young echoed the sentiment that the Saints should gather in communities. He decried the "injudicious movement" of settling on scattered farms or up canyons on whatever piece of land caught their fancy. He said that it "would give their enemies an opportunity to disturb their peace and perhaps endanger the lives of many, which is a thing we desire to avoid. God has given us wisdom to preserve ourselves, and if the brethren will strictly adhere to council, God will overrule all things for their good."[6]

The plat for the city of Zion provided the template for Salt Lake City and most other settlements in the Great Basin, but on a much smaller scale. Just as the city of Zion was to provide social benefits, the village system facilitated group life, knitting people together into a cohesive whole.[7] Mormon farm villages were unique in the West not only because the church was the only faith to move its entire organization west, but also because the Homestead Act (1862), under which much of the land outside of the Great Basin was claimed, required people to live on their land to gain title to it. St. Thomas residents did not apply for ownership of their land through the Homestead Act, but formed their settlement according to the Mormon pattern.

The exact measurements of town plats might not have been an article of faith, but forming farming villages was. In 1838 Joseph Smith specifically said that "it was the duty of the brethren to come into the cities and build and live, and carry on their farms out of the cities, according to the order of God." This made the act of creating new towns and inhabiting them virtually a sacrament on the land. It provided security, allowed the retaining of church organization, promoted social contact, and allowed for cooperative work arrangements.[8]

There was one other way that St. Thomas fitted firmly Mormon settlement patterns: the Saints located it in an area most whites initially spurned. The Saints did not rejoice in inhabiting poor lands per se, but believed they were fulfilling prophecy by doing so. In the Old Testament of the Bible, Isaiah 35:1 reads, "The wilderness and the solitary place shall be glad for them; and the desert shall rejoice, and blossom as a rose." This is a precondition to the Second Coming of Christ. They believed that by settling in "desert" places and exerting themselves to make them blossom, they were hastening the coming of the Lord. From a practical standpoint, they had been driven out of Kirtland, Ohio; Independence, Missouri; and Nauvoo, Illinois; settling in areas nobody else wanted forestalled a similar expulsion from the Great Basin.

Were it not for mineral resources, the Mormons may have been unchallenged in the area. On September 11, 1861, the *Deseret News* described much of the area that became the state of Utah as "measurably valueless, excepting for nomadic purposes, hunting grounds for the Indians, and to hold the world together." A discourse by apostle George Q. Cannon in 1873 is instructive. He told the Saints that "good countries are not for us. . . . [T]he worst places in the land we can probably get and we must develop them." They should thank God, even if all they had was a "little oasis in the desert where few can settle."[9] After all, every other crop was secondary to growing Saints.

Brigham Young, in numerous sermons, indicated that the Great Basin was uniquely adapted for that production, even if nothing else would readily take root.

No matter the condition of the land, the Saints wanted to ensure that their control of St. Thomas remained unchallenged. Four days after Smith's party arrived on the Muddy, Brigham Young received Anson Call's report of the area. Call reported a fine body of land at the confluence of the Virgin and Muddy Rivers that was equal to any land in the Utah Territory. The area would comfortably support three hundred families. Young, writing to Daniel H. Wells of the First Presidency, stated they must take all the eligible spots, "as we have no wish to see outside parties come in and take possession of the best places and reap the fruits of our toil." Young believed this would surely be the case once other parties discovered that they were going to route all their shipping through the area. In addition to settlement, George A. Smith in the Utah territorial legislature oversaw the passage of a memorial to Congress asking the attachment of the Muddy to Utah, since they understood it to be part of Arizona.[10] The uncertainty about under whose jurisdiction St. Thomas lay proved very troublesome during the entire time the town was part of the Muddy Mission.

In addition to the settlers officially called to the Muddy, church leaders encouraged any who desired to be part of the new settlement to go south. Brigham Young answered many letters in 1865 from people who wanted to take advantage of a fresh start and warmer weather on the Muddy. He also fielded many letters from bishops asking what they should tell people who wanted a release from their current assignments so they could go south. President Young generally granted the person permission to go and assist in settling the country. He advised them to travel to St. George, where apostle Erastus Snow would give them further instruction. If they could not leave immediately, Young counseled them to send an agent on their behalf to select and secure land and put in grain to ensure food was available upon their arrival. Many were no doubt heartened by Anson Call's positive description of the Muddy.

Regardless of why people came, by May 1865 between forty and fifty men with families arrived in St. Thomas. There were enough people on the Muddy that church leadership created the St. Joseph Branch, with Warren Foote as branch president. St. Joseph is now known as Logandale. The first natural increase began to affect the population in the summer of 1865, when

Margaret Ellen Johnston, daughter of William James and Ellen Turks Johnston, was born. Thomas S. Smith blessed the child on August 6.[11]

The calling of missionaries to St. Thomas and the Muddy was not isolated
to the October conference of 1864. Erastus Snow, apostle and leader of the
Southern Utah Mission, complained that most of the original "wealthy" missionaries had neither gone south nor sent replacements. Those sent brought
only the barest of necessities. In early 1865, Brigham Young sent letters to
bishops of various settlements asking them if any ward members wanted to
join the new colonization effort. In March 1865, he wrote to James Martineau,
indicating that he and other leaders were anxious to have many families
settle on all the lands available for settlement.

President Young periodically issued individual callings. In the fall of
1866, Neils Ipson received one of these callings to settle in St. Thomas and
assist in building up the Muddy Mission. Ipson immediately began selling
everything he had in Manti, Utah, except for necessities transportable by
ox train. He took with him his first wife, Georgine, and her children and his
third wife, Inger Kerstine, who was pregnant during the journey.[12]

It is significant that Ipson took his first wife to the Muddy, because the
1870 census seems to indicate that this was not the normal practice. The
average fifteen-year disparity between the ages of husbands and wives sug-
gests that "first families" generally remained in the North, while men took
younger wives to the Muddy. At St. Joseph, the median age for men was
thirty-nine and for women twenty-four. At nearby Overton, the respective
figures were forty-nine and thirty-five.[13]

When individual callings did not provide enough new settlers, President Young issued 158 new calls in the October 1867 conference. Most were
young, unmarried men; many were recently returned missionaries who had
labored in Europe. Church leadership believed they would inject the settlement with new life. President Young asked those who were single to marry
and take their wives with them, so Salt Lake City experienced a small boom
in marriages. Two of the women married in this group who went south were
daughters of President Young. Young was pleased that so many responded
to the call. He wrote to Franklin D. Richards two weeks after the issuing of
the calls, stating that many of the newly called were almost ready to depart.
He rejoiced in the "alacrity with which they respond to any call that may
be made upon them whether it is to preach the gospel, to gather the poor,
or do anything connected with the work of God abroad; or to build up new

settlements and to perform any of the multifarious duties devolving upon them in this new country."[14]

Despite President Young's optimism, the *Journal History* reports that of those called at that conference, only about 80 reached the Muddy. Many of the newly arrived missionaries were experienced cotton growers, which was a great benefit to the existing settlements. Although the established missionaries were willing to share their land, many of these new settlers were rebellious, rejected the council to settle in established areas, and formed their own settlement on the Upper Muddy. Another 150 missionaries received calls at the October 1868 General Conference. Rather than attempting to infuse the mission with youth again, Brigham Young called "men of weight" who were well respected in the places from which they hailed. This round of calls was more effective than previous ones. This is clear from reports received in January 1869, which claimed that most of the missionaries called at the conference had arrived. The messenger passed others heading to the Muddy while carrying the report north.[15]

St. Thomas did not remain the only town on the Muddy for very long, but it continued as the principal town. Thomas S. Smith was the acting bishop and high priest over the settlements on the Muddy, and since he lived in St. Thomas, all major communication went through that community. The town served as the base of explorations for the Mormons. Gentiles used it as a principal supply stop as well. When George M. Wheeler of the Army Corps of Engineers explored the lower canyons area of the Colorado, he traveled to the mouth of the Muddy in September 1869 for supplies.[16]

St. Thomas played a role as a transportation and information center in the southern Great Basin for many expeditions, including John Wesley Powell's exploration of the Colorado. On August 30, 1869, when Powell's party emerged from the Grand Wash, the outlet for the Grand Canyon, some Mormon residents were there to meet them. Powell recorded that a Mr. Asa and his two sons were far less surprised to see the group than he was to see them. Leaders in St. Thomas received a report that Powell's party was lost, and church leaders in Salt Lake City wanted St. Thomas residents to watch for any fragments or remnants of the party. Once Powell received the news that a Colonel Head had sent mail addressed to members of the expedition to St. Thomas, he immediately dispatched a Paiute runner to the town to get it. Powell's men were most anxious to get their mail, since their last mail stop was in Green River City, three and a half months earlier.[17]

The next day, the runner returned with a letter from Bishop James Leit-head, saying he was bringing two or three men and supplies for the exhausted explorers. Leithead arrived that evening to a very welcome reception, as he brought three dozen melons and other luxury items for Powell and his men. Powell and his men went on to St. Thomas, where Frederick S. Dellenbaugh, who was the artist and topographer for the Powell expedition, found himself very impressed by the town and its people. He observed, "As pioneers, the Mormons were superior to any class I have ever come in contact with, their idea being home-making and not skimming the cream off the country with a six-shooter and a whiskey bottle." Butter, milk, cheese, and vegetables were readily available, as opposed to Gentile towns, where if such items were available, they were canned. Indeed, the empty tin was the chief decoration in Gentile frontier towns; Mormon towns looked much better when compared with "the entire absence of any attempt at arrangement at order, or to start fruit or shade trees, or do any other sensible thing." Rather, "Gentile frontier town[s were] a ghastly hodge-podge of shacks in the midst of a sea of refuse."[18] Possibly his favorable report was influenced by the fact that St. Thomas was the first "civilization" he had seen in months. Even if this is the case, many of those traveling through the town on the early Arrowhead Trail highway repeated his sentiments years later.

In 1869 the church decided to increase the amount of "civilization" on the Muddy by making communication between St. Thomas and the rest of the church's settlements easier. In April Brigham Young asked the Saints at St. George to put up telegraph poles to connect with the settlements on the Muddy. He promised that if they erected the poles, the church would provide wire and instruments to complete the line. In June Erastus Snow traveled to St. Thomas to introduce the proposal to the Saints on the Muddy. Snow also asked the Saints to purchase stock in the cotton factory. Residents passed a resolution to build their portion of the telegraph from St. Thomas north and appointed Andrew Gibbons and Joseph W. Young to locate the line and apportion the cost out to all the settlements. They also subscribed eleven hundred dollars toward the cotton factory.[19] There are no records that the telegraph line was ever built.

Although it was true that the Muddy did have water and arable land, there were significant disadvantages to living there, the weather being chief among them. Extreme summer heat was pervasive, causing everyone to suffer. Summertime temperatures could top 120 degrees. In the official history of the Muddy Mission, assistant church historian Andrew Jensen wrote that watering carrots in the morning would cook them by noon, causing the skin to slip off when pulled out of the ground. Men working in the field would put fresh coffee grounds in a canteen and hang it on a bush. By noon the coffee was ready. Schoolgirls would run until their feet hurt, throw down their bonnet or apron, and stand on it until their feet cooled. Jensen said that he perspired so much that after his overalls dried when he took them off at night, they would nearly stand on their own from all the minerals and salt in them. A swamp nearby St. Thomas meant mosquitoes and malaria. Combined with the heat, this meant that the missionaries "had to bake the days [they] didn't shake," referring to malaria's symptom of shaking.[20] Adding to their discomfort were occasional outbreaks of influenza, whooping cough, and other maladies.

There was little reprieve from the heat at night. The setting of the sun simply made it dark, not cool. Abraham Kimball wrote that in order to sleep, he would climb on top of a shed, thus escaping the scorpions, tarantulas, and rattlesnakes. Unfortunately, there was no escaping the mosquitoes. Samuel Claridge said that in order to escape the heat, he would go out and lie naked in the ditch that ran through their lot. By morning, he almost felt worse than he had when he lay down, having slept in a muddy ditch all night.[21]

The oppressive heat also proved very hard on the animals. One woman gave up raising chickens because the hot sand cooked the eggs nearly as fast as the hens laid them, though the hens were willing to sit on them until they boiled. She related her attempt to rescue some of the eggs, where she set three eggs up on the mantle with the intent of using them in the evening. Distracted by the arrival of her husband, she forgot about the eggs. She later remembered the eggs when she found a chick on the mantle that had incubated in the ambient air. Dogs scratched frantically in the sand for places to cool their burning feet, while the chickens threw themselves on their backs to wave their feet in the air in an attempt to cool off.[22] Heat was not the only problem. High winds destroyed gardens and filled in irrigation ditches with sand. The blowing sand combined with the heat made the area almost unbearable.

The summer sun was capable of doing more than simply making people miserable. In his *Annals,* Bleak recorded that on June 12, 1869, a horse wandered into the camp of some people digging a well. The laborers fed and watered the horse and tied it up, thinking that it had wandered from its owners. One of the workers, William Webb, went out with one of his mules and found a boy lying dead about a half mile from the camp. His face and body were so badly bloated from exposure to the heat of the sun that he thwarted identification efforts. Beside the boy were an empty canteen and a dry gallon keg. Webb buried the boy and put up a headboard to mark the place. Soon after, residents discovered that James Davidson, his wife, and his son had left St. Thomas for St. George. Along the way, their wagon had lost a wheel along a waterless stretch. Would-be rescuers found Mr. and Mrs. Davidson lying together under a blanket stretched over two cacti where they had camped while their son went for water. James Leithead, who at this time was the bishop at St. Thomas, sent a party of men either to retrieve or to bury the Davidsons.

Those who were not members of the LDS Church were also aware of how uncomfortable it could be on the Muddy. When Italian revolutionaries forced Pope Pius IX from Rome, Secretary of State Seward offered him asylum in the United States. One Salt Lake reporter went further and offered the pope and his entourage a farm on the Muddy. Historian John Townley wrote, "One senses an inference that the Muddy was the ultimate in earthly damnation that could be provided Pius IX." The anti-Mormon *Salt Lake Tribune* characterized the Muddy as a "Siberia for troublemakers from better lands in the North."[23]

Despite the weather, there were Gentiles who were very interested in creating a presence on the Muddy. A group of San Francisco merchants contemplated the sale of stock to create a steam navigation company to cultivate a possible market there. Church leaders expressed concern over this plan. Brigham Young said church leaders desired to take up every eligible spot on the Muddy River, the Colorado River, and at Las Vegas, "so as to prevent stragglers who are drifting around that country from securing land and speculating and profiting by our operations and toil." When word reached President Young that there were Gentiles trying to settle near Callville, he sent people to claim all remaining land and to try to convince the non-Mormons to leave.[24]

In 1868 the Union Pacific Railroad announced the commencement of a rail line that would start at Washoe and go through the Pahranagat Valley, down the Muddy, and on to Prescott, Arizona; the announcement met with consternation. Planners contemplated the rail line as a means of accessing the Southern Pacific Railroad at Kingman, Arizona. No doubt completion of the transcontinental railroad in May 1869 stalled progress on the route before it reached St. Thomas. Some Gentile traffic did pass through St. Thomas, as the machinery that was used to process ore on the Pahranagat traveled through the town.[25]

Even though the summers were oppressive, most Mormons called to the Muddy did not complain about conditions to their church leaders. Regardless of how they might have felt, "murmuring" showed a lack of faith. Whatever burdens were borne, they were borne for God. Others liked the heat, or at least tolerated it better, and thrived. Regardless of which description fitted individual settlers, most agreed the winters were pleasant. The missionaries were encouraged by their prospects for the future and sent President Young a glowing report in February 1868. According to the letter, the sun was shining, and the thermometer read 55 degrees. The men could work without their coats, and the only need for fire was to cook their food. It was a "delightful climate," though fuel was scarce.[26] The scarcity of fuel was one of the few negative references to the Muddy that Brigham Young openly acknowledged.

It was during this time of "delightful climate" that settlers established St. Thomas in January 1865. The first building constructed was a fort, as was customary. In addition to putting land to the plow that had never before supported intensive, European-style agriculture, the Saints also set about familiarizing themselves with their new surroundings. In April 1865, the stake presidency from St. George, apostle Erastus Snow, Marius Ensign, James G. Bleak, and James Cragun, came to St. Thomas to visit the new settlement. The day after they arrived, President Snow and Thomas Smith traveled up the valley to explore. About two miles above St. Thomas, they came upon a meadow they estimated to be about one thousand acres. Two miles farther up, the Saints found another promising meadow of six hundred acres. The first meadow they came upon must have been appealing indeed, because in February 1866, residents surveyed it in preparation for relocating the town. The second survey followed the same plan as the first, with eighty-five one-acre lots and the same number of two-and-a-half-acre vineyard lots and five-acre farm lots. Bleak reported that by early March, people were moving to the newly surveyed St. Thomas.[27] It is this second meadow where the rusting and decaying remains of St. Thomas lie today.

Construction proved difficult due to the lack of wood and other building materials. In 1870 Bleak indicated that the cost of getting lumber to the lower Muddy was twenty dollars per one hundred board feet.[28] At that price, one would get only 18.75 eight-foot, two-by-four-inch boards for twenty dollars, which is enough to frame only one fifteen-foot wall using modern construction methods. Because of costs, most settlers chose to build houses out of adobe bricks, which Mormons used extensively elsewhere. Adobe houses did require some lumber for the door and window frames, but much less than required by a frame house. Floors, at least at first, were usually dirt, but packed so hard they could almost be scrubbed. Women would often inscribe intricate designs into the dirt floors to give the impression that the walking surface was really just an earth-colored carpet.

Adobe bricks were not the only building materials in use. Henry and Mary Maudsley lived in St. Thomas for four years in a tent. They walled up the sides and put a fireplace at one end. To protect the roof of the tent, they built a bowery of willows over it. The tent of Hannah Sharp had a floor of straw, which she changed frequently. Sometimes Sister Sharp would say, when visiting someone's home, "Well, girls, I must go home now. I have to put down a new carpet this morning." Settlers constructed the first church meetinghouse out of woven willows. It had a dirt floor and two square holes without glass in the back for light.[29]

Charles Pears Smith had a novel approach to home building. He built his shelter by digging a trench in the earth, then placing upright posts closely together in the trench. He wove wet strips of cowhide between the posts near the top, which held the posts tightly once dried. Smith then covered the posts with plaster, which provided protection from both the heat and the cold. He made the roof by stretching small poles from wall to wall and then covering the poles with willows. Finally, he wove bear grass throughout the roof and then spread a coat of mud on top.[30]

Other Saints found different methods to create a workable roof. Helen Gibbons recorded that some would go to the swampy areas of the Muddy and gather cattails and tie them in bunches six inches in diameter. These cattails grew up to twelve feet tall, so they were long enough to make a good roof by piling them on and tying them in place. The cattail roof shed snow and rain, keeping the occupants dry. For all the creativeness of St. Thomas residents, there were some traditional buildings. The new meetinghouse had a roof of handmade wooden shingles.[31]

Despite the few buildings like the meetinghouse, many felt that St. Thomas was a rough-looking place. One missionary described it as "a little group of adobe huts with willow and mud roofs mussed together into a fort, pitiful attempts at wheat and corn fields; not a tree to impede the direct rays of the sun." The lack of timber made it hard to construct fences out of poles, so residents created corrals by piling mesquite bushes to enclose an area. The lack of wood presented a problem for cooking. There was some desert willow, but the main source of fuel was mesquite. The settlers paid Paiutes to dig the entire tree up, roots and all, and dry it out to burn it. The work was hard, and a good worker could manage seven or eight a day. For this work, the Paiutes received a cup of flour per root.[32]

Church leaders recognized that many would find St. Thomas less than desirable, but realized that it was the best place to settle in the area. Brigham Young felt that despite the deficiencies, industry and perseverance were the only requirements to make the place a desirable one to dwell. He wrote to Joseph Murdock, "It is no new thing for the Saints to contend with and overcome the obstacles" that the Muddy had to offer. President Young based his opinion on the reports of others, as he did not visit the area until 1870.

For nearly a decade before the church planted a town on the Muddy, the Moapa Paiutes had asked for the Saints to become their neighbors.[33] The Paiutes asked Las Vegas-bound missionaries in 1855 to settle there, and many Paiutes received baptism at the hands of the elders. Nevertheless, many of the problems that the residents of St. Thomas encountered were because the Moapa Valley had inhabitants when the Saints arrived. There were understandable tensions, since the situation created by the founding of the town was that of two sizable groups of culturally dissimilar people living in close proximity. There are no indications that church leaders expected the settlers to proselyte the Paiutes as in Las Vegas, but frictions arose because of other matters. Three months after the arrival of Thomas Smith, some of these tensions came to a head.

Toward the end of Erastus Snow's visit in April 1865, his company received a visit from To-ish-obe, the principal chief of the Muddy band of Paiutes, and a number of his men. To-ish-obe first addressed Snow's company in a very angry and excited manner. President Snow listened patiently to the interpretation given by Andrew Gibbons and replied mildly. Snow's subdued manner helped defuse the tense situation. To-ish-obe told Snow that some of the Santa Clara Paiutes who lived near St. George and Santa Clara had sent word that "Snow and some of his men were going to the Muddy and poison the water and kill off all the Indians." Snow assured the chief that these were not his intentions, and the meeting ended peacefully. Bleak reported that the false report had been circulated because the Paiutes from the St. George area had experienced some bad business dealings with some Mormons and were resentful.[34]

The Paiutes certainly deserve some blame for difficulties experienced between the two groups. Many of those problems, however, are traceable to attitudes that the Mormons held toward Native Americans. Joseph W. Young's correspondence with the *Deseret News* is illustrative. In 1868 he wrote, "In the early history of our Utah settlements these Indians were considered about the worst specimens of the race. They lived almost in a state of nudity, and were among the worst thieves on the continent." Another observer wrote, "The Indians on the Rio Virgin and Muddy are the most low and contemptible I ever saw and show the most degraded and dishonest disposition. They are worse than the Otoes & Omahas & I believe they are more treacherous and fickle." Young, at least, recognized that the Mormons deserved some blame for poor relationships. He reported that the Native Americans, when the letter was sent, were peaceful, and "perhaps might continue so, if there were no foolish white men; but unfortunately there were too many of that kind."[35]

Darius Clement knew one such man in St. Thomas. This man stole some ammunition from the Paiutes and "degraded himself to their level." Speaking of the incident, Brigham Young said that he would not whip an Indian any sooner than he would a white man if the white man was guilty of the same thing. The white man should "receive more & severer lashes of the black snake, because he had been taught better." Another culturally insensitive white man was Captain R. N. Fenton, whom the government sent in 1869 to be the agent for the Paiutes living on the Muddy. They looked on him with such contempt that he had to threaten to open fire on them in order to get their attention.[36]

Food was the source of many of the confrontations between residents of St. Thomas and the Paiutes. Some of them were minor. Orville Cox recorded one such incident in his journal. His wife, Elvira, was ironing a shirt with the door to the house open. They had no stove to heat the irons, so she was using long-handled fire shovels, bottom up, over a pile of coals, and she would use one while the other heated. A "big buck Indian" wearing a G-string and breechclout came to the door and demanded bread. Elvira gave him three small biscuits. He demanded more, but she told him there was none. He then demanded the shirt, which she refused, saying that it was her son's only shirt and he was in bed while she ironed it. The man bent to pick up the shirt, so Elvira picked up one of the shovels and whacked his bare backside. From then on, his friends knew him as the "buck that was branded by a squaw."

Other confrontations were more severe. One day a white boy killed a rabbit for food. The Paiutes believed that all the wild game belonged to them and demanded that the boy be shot, or at least punished in some way. The settlers held a council with the Paiutes and agreed that they would not kill any of their wild animals if they would agree not to kill any of the white men's cattle. They still demanded that the boy, Walt, be shot. Walt was able to shoot some wild ducks that the Paiutes accepted instead.[37]

Not so easily resolved was a raid on the settlers' cattle. Because cattle left to roam were sometimes picked off and eaten by the Paiutes, the settlers had taken to herding all their livestock onto an island in the Muddy at night. The *Annals* recorded that one morning in February 1866, the settlers discovered that their neighbors had improvised a bridge to the island for the livestock to pass over. They were able to escape with all the cattle and horses, about sixty head. The Paiutes had pulled up all their crops and had taken every man, woman, and child out of the valley. They had even buried containers of water out along the trail so they could escape quickly. The loss of all their work animals made it very difficult for the settlers to complete their work.

Eventually, the Paiutes began to filter back into the valley after the incident. Warren Foote recorded how the matter was eventually resolved. St. Thomas leaders called up Old Captain Thomas to explain their actions. Thomas said that the band that lived over the Timber Mountains "prevailed" upon them to assist in the theft. Captain Rufus, another leader, and himself were opposed to the theft, but fearing reprisals fled with the actual thieves. After their successful escape, the other band took all the food from the Paiutes from the Muddy and left them to starve. Thomas and those who followed him decided to give themselves up to the Mormons so they could return to their homes. Brother Thomas S. Smith spoke with them, saying that the Saints had settled there to do the Paiutes good, that we were their friends, and reminded them of the good done for them. The theft of the teams had deprived the missionaries the ability to plow the land and raise grain to feed their women and children, who might now go hungry. Foote recalled that when Brother Smith's words were interpreted to him, "tears ran down old Captain Thomas' cheeks and they seemed fully to sense the crime they had committed, and to throw themselves upon our mercies."[38]

Some of the culprits received severe punishment. Old Thomas, who was chief of the band near the California Road, To-ish-obe, who was chief of the Muddy band, and another chief met together and decided that two of their men who had stolen horses and cattle were outlaws. The chiefs delivered Co-quap, one of the guilty parties, to St. Thomas for execution. By one account, his execution was cruel. The Mormons took him two miles out of town and let him loose. They shot at him jumping and running, nearly making his escape before falling prey to Mormon bullets. According to another source, St. Thomas residents simply hanged him; this explanation seems more in line with Mormon attitudes toward Native Americans.[39]

To forestall difficulties in the future, Price Nelson recorded in his journal that the Paiutes made a treaty that whoever stole and was caught was to be whipped, five lashes for the first offense and doubled every time after that. Nevertheless, To-ish-obe had a hard time getting his people to refrain from theft and sabotage of the settlers' crops. The chief requested that Andrew Gibbons come and talk to the Paiute men, because they would listen to him. Even though To-ish-obe was not always able to control his people, the settlers on the Muddy were grateful for his moderating influence.[40]

Part of why To-ish-obe had a hard time controlling his people is because he was a chief in only the loosest sense of the word. He was the one in charge of his band, but only because his band chose to follow him. If his people did not like what he was doing, they were free to follow someone else or strike out on their own. If a chief pushed too hard, he could easily lose his position. The rigidly hierarchical Mormons did not understand this and expected the chiefs to be able to give orders in the same way a bishop would and expect compliance. Mormons did not understand that any "treaty" made with a particular chief may not result in the compliance of the people in his band.[41]

It is unsurprising, then, that during 1866, the moderating influence of To-ish-obe proved insufficient to keep the peace. That year saw a general uneasiness and anger among Native Americans due to the Black Hawk War. Utah's Black Hawk War lasted from 1865 to 1872. Named after Ute chief Antonga Black Hawk, the war was a series of battles, skirmishes, raids, and killings between the Mormon settlers in central and southern Utah and the Ute, Paiutes, and Navajo. Native American belligerents responded to Mormon pressure on their hunting, fishing, and camping areas; sought revenge for personal insults; and generally sought to discourage further outside settlement. The Ute felt particularly aggrieved by the lack of promised supplies and the resultant starvation at the Uintah Indian Reservation during the winter of 1864-65. Mormon settlers retaliated against repeated livestock raids and constant begging by their Native neighbors. During the war, the Paiutes on the Muddy became bolder, and it was more difficult to maintain relations with them. In an attempt to normalize relations with area bands, Erastus Snow convened a meeting at St. Joseph with Tut-se-gavits, chief of the Santa Clara band; To-ish-obe, principal chief of the Muddy band; William, chief of the Colorado band; Farmer, chief of the St. Thomas band; Frank, chief of the Simondsville band; Rufus, chief of the Muddy Springs band above the California Road; and Thomas, chief of the band at the Narrows of the Muddy. Sixty-four braves from the seven bands accompanied the chiefs to the meeting.[42] President Snow spoke at length through interpreters, and a good feeling prevailed at the meeting.

A meeting with the Paiute bands was not the only reason President Snow traveled south from St. George. He received a letter from President Young and his councillors on May 20, 1866, instructing him to make the necessary preparations in each settlement to protect them from Native American attacks. The letter required 150 to 500 "good and efficient" men be called in each settlement for the militia. If it became necessary to travel outside of the settlement, no parties of one or two should leave alone, but should travel in a well-armed party or be escorted by armed guards, as "the careless manner in which men have traveled from place to place . . . should be stopped." Any abandoned settlement should have their house logs and fence poles buried to prevent their destruction. The Saints should "adopt measures from this time forward that not another drop of your blood, or the blood of anyone belonging to you, shall be shed by the Indians and keep your stock so securely that not another horse, mule, ox, cow, sheep, or even calf shall fall in their hands and the war will soon be stopped." Any settlement not abandoned should have a strong fort erected, and all the people should move into it. To protect livestock, the letter stipulated the construction of strong corrals. When it became necessary to send their animals out to graze, an armed guard should accompany them. Bleak indicated in the *Annals* that the same rules applied for men working in the fields.

Pursuant to Young's instructions, Snow organized a battalion of the Nauvoo Legion for the Muddy consisting of 93 men, rank and file, with Thomas

S. Smith as major. He also divided the Muddy into two areas for protection. In case of a conflict with Paiutes, all settlers on the south end of the valley were to travel to St. Thomas and band together for protection. Snow designated Mill Point as the meeting place in the North. St. Joseph residents, who were in the middle, were at liberty to choose where they would go.[43]

No major confrontations occurred on the Muddy, despite the scare in August 1866. In a letter to Thomas Smith, Brigham Young shared some information he had received regarding the movement of Native Americans in the area. Kanosh, the chief of the Pahvant band of the Ute, which was the only large group of Ute that did not participate in the Black Hawk War, carried the warning. He said that the Piedes (Southern Paiutes on the Arizona Strip) told him that two sons of a slain Navajo chief were preparing to descend on the settlements in the South with 6,000 warriors and reclaim all the land from St. George to Beaver. Young called this an "Indian story," but one that called for observation. He called on settlers to push forward their efforts to defend the settlements on the Muddy, sparing no pain to secure the area. President Young also indicated that he would attempt to raise more people to settle on the Muddy to strengthen it.[44]

Although there was no general warfare, occasional confrontations occurred. Delaun Mills Cox recorded one such confrontation in his history. Some Paiutes killed a cow, and the herdsmen reported it. Men from St. Thomas, Overton, and St. Joseph went to confront them and demand payment for the cow. The guilty parties replied that they would fight first and called their brothers to arms. Cox reported:

> All night long the Indians kept up the pow-wow and war dance on a little knoll not far from town. Early the next morning the men all gathered [to organize.] The Indians came down a few at a time, twanging their bow strings, anxious and waiting to shoot. A few of them in front had guns. There were about fifty who came forward but there were around seventy-five in the whole bunch. Finally their big chief, Frank put in his appearance. Andrew Gibbons stood on the wagon tongue and began talking peace, and the Indians were about to give in when one young buck began twanging his bow string again and raising his tomahawk. This was all that was needed to stir up the fighting blood of the Indians, and the Captain said, "No, we'll fight." . . . [There was then some maneuvering for position.] "Don't shoot," commanded Pratt, for just then an old Indian stepped out calling, "Hole-on, hole-on, hole-on," and Captain Frank began waving his blanket which signified

surrender. When the Indians saw that the white men really meant business they didn't feel so brave, so the battle, though a silent one, ended without bloodshed, but it was a close call.[45]

The Black Hawk War continued until 1872, but the Moapa Paiutes stopped participating in 1867, and relations between St. Thomas residents and the Paiutes returned to a semblance of normalcy. In order to maintain that peace, President Young advised that no Saint should attempt to establish a settlement north of the California Road, I-15 today. From that point on, Erastus Snow advised new settlers that despite their feelings toward Paiutes, it was much more effective to "shoot them with biscuits" than with bullets. There were other instances of the Paiutes taking and killing horses and cattle, but the warlike feeling that had prevailed on the Muddy dissipated for a while. Unfortunately, another confrontation in late 1870, right before the Saints left the Muddy, led to the decision that thieves caught in the act of stealing faced execution.[46]

Not all the interactions between St. Thomas residents and the Paiutes were negative. The Mormons tried to teach them better farming methods to increase their food supply with disappointing results. The Paiutes, however, were an important source of labor for the Saints. Joseph W. Young wrote that of all the tribes he had experience with, the Paiutes were the best workers. They were hired to do housework, haul wood, do construction, and for agricultural work. Payment for services rendered was usually in food. For picking cotton, a Paiute woman received a yard of calico and three cakes of bread per day. For washing for several hours, their pay consisted of a level pint of flour.[47]

Working and living in close proximity to each other did generate some moments of understanding between the two groups. Hannah Sharp noticed that the Paiutes had a novel way of avoiding sunstroke. They would wind their hair around their heads and plaster it with wet mud, which they allowed to dry. As the mud chipped off, they added more mud. Others just found their prejudices confirmed. One sister writing to her friend stated, "There is no lack of company, for I have about a dozen dirty-looking Indian visitors every day, and they manage to stay all day sneaking around, and watching out, as though you were stealing. I have engaged one to wash for me, what do you think of our hired help? Is it not a fine prospect, to think of spending one's days with such associates?"[48]

On at least one occasion, amusement was the result of cultural misunderstanding. Joseph W. Young related the following story in the *Deseret News*.
One Paiute man decided he wanted the wife of another man, to which, of
course, the second man objected. To decide the matter, all the friends of the
two men gathered to fight for the woman. After laying their clothes and
weapons to the side, the two sides fought until a victor emerged and led the
woman to his willow shade. The woman had no voice in the proceedings.
Sometimes, when the two sides got tired of beating each other, they would
grab the woman and engage in a tug-of-war, almost killing the poor woman.
The Saints tried to get the Paiutes to moderate these "barbarities" as much
as possible, but in at least one case, a Mormon's attempt to intervene was
significantly misunderstood. Joseph W. Young recalled:

> One man, who is by the way, a pretty hard man to handle, got his sympathies
> excited by seeing some twenty Indians pulling at a little squaw, and he went up to
> try and make them desist, when they thought he wanted a hand in the fight, and
> they all turned on him, but he soon whipped the whole of them. They gave him
> peaceable possession, and all hands cheered for the *wyno* Mormon. He turned the
> prize over to the brave, who, he thought had the best claim: still the young lady
> claims to be his squaw, and says she is just living out on permission.[49]

In 1869 government action altered the basic relationship between the
Mormons and the Paiutes. The Mormons took very seriously President
Young's advice that it was easier to feed the Native Americans than to fight
them. They showed this repeatedly by their distribution of a lot of blan-
kets, shirts, agricultural tools, and other items to the Paiutes. Captain R. N.
Fenton arrived on the Muddy to take up his duties as Indian agent. Fenton
believed in taking a different approach than the Mormons, disrupting the
relationship that had worked fairly well up to that point. He believed that
the Paiutes were ready to go onto a reservation because they were so poor
and starving, and reservation life would ensure the meeting of their basic
needs. He recommended the creation of a reservation on the Upper Muddy,
an area that the Saints had left to the Paiutes anyway. Many of the Saints
were worried that instead of placing the reservation on the Upper Muddy,
Captain Fenton would recommend the designation of the entire Muddy as a
reservation, thus breaking up the settlements. The uncertainty threw them
into a "state of suspense & anxiety & clouded their future prospects which
hitherto seemed bright." The anxiety proved unfounded in December 1869,

as Captain Fenton received word from the Indian Department of the acceptance of the Upper Muddy as the site for the reservation. In February 1870, Fenton moved his headquarters from St. Thomas to Hiko, as it was "nearer the central part of this tribe of Indians, than St. Thomas, and more convenient for communications." Five months later, Fenton moved to Pioche, as it was "more convenient for the transaction of the business connected with [the] Agency." In reality, he moved to Pioche so he could participate in the mining boom there, neglecting his duties as agent.[50]

St. Thomas residents did not spend all their time worrying about relations with the Paiutes. They had to work to support themselves and their families. The primary occupation of St. Thomas residents was farming. Bleak recorded that in April 1865, several farmers broke ground and put in crops. He listed that Thomas S. Smith had seven acres of wheat, two of barley, and one of oats. John Bankhead, from Wellsville, in Cache Valley, Utah, had planted ten acres of wheat and two of oats. Robert Harris, from Davis County, planted nine acres of wheat, one acre of barley, and one acre of oats. Henry Nebeker from Payson, Utah County, had ten acres of wheat. Many of the men had gone north shortly after arriving to retrieve their families or to get food. Bleak mentions only thirty-three acres under the plow, but the Mormons surveyed nine hundred acres for farmland, and six hundred of those acres belonged to settlers. The one thousand acres of meadowland remained unsurveyed.[51]

The first year of farming seemed promising for the new community. Cotton grew very well on the Muddy, and by October the agriculturalists looked forward to a good crop. They were not disappointed, either, as all the settlements on the Muddy raised five thousand pounds of cotton that first year. Andrew Gibbons was particularly enthusiastic about the prospects of agriculture at St. Thomas. He said, "All that we need, to make this part of the desert blossom like the rose, is the men and means."[52]

What the desert really needed to blossom like a rose was not just men and means, but water. In addition to surveying the land for farming, the Saints wasted no time digging irrigation canals to water their new fields. In an August 1865 report to Wilford Woodruff, apostle and president of the Deseret Agricultural and Manufacturing Society, St. Thomas residents reported the construction of a three-mile-long, eight-foot-wide, two-and-a-half-foot-deep canal. They used teams and scrapers as much as possible, but much of the work required a pick and a shovel. The estimated cost of labor and materials totaled $3,840. Another $1,160 worth of smaller canals was under construction at the time of the report.[53]

In 1866 St. Thomas residents built a dam north of their settlement to raise the level of the water in the river so that it would feed their ditch. First, they had to dig a canal around a swamp so they could get to a suitable dam site. Warren Foote and twenty others from St. Joseph went south to help in the construction. Foote helped the St. Thomas residents lay out ditches along the streets to facilitate water delivery for garden lots.[54]

Starting in 1868, St. Thomas began to have serious problems with water. As the population increased on the Muddy, so did the demand for the finite resource. The canal that the residents of St. Joseph dug to supply their community with water presented the biggest problem for the town downstream. About two hundred yards of it ran through sandy soil, and up to 90 percent of the water that ran through it seeped into the ground. This new canal greatly diminished the amount of water that made it downstream to St. Thomas.[55] In communities not controlled by the church, such a situation would certainly have led to litigation, and rightly so. As leaders in Salt Lake directed both communities, all parties involved sought another solution.

The lack of water is traceable to other reasons besides the actions of upstream residents. The swamp to the north of St. Thomas took much of the water that made it past St. Joseph's canal. It also bred mosquitoes while keeping land out of cultivation. To overcome this problem, residents dug a ditch ten miles long, six feet wide, and two and a half feet deep to drain the swamp. The completion of the ditch allayed the fears of scarcity of water for St. Thomas residents. Their confidence was conditional, though. They recognized that St. Thomas had reached its population capacity.[56]

Even their conditional optimism was not well founded. The year 1869 was one of drought, and the lack of water resulted in very poor yields in every crop. The drought required new solutions. Speaking at St. Thomas in December 1869, Erastus Snow proposed a solution. He said that the Muddy should be totally diverted into two canals, one on each side of the valley—one to St. Joseph on the east side and the other to St. Thomas on the west. Each settlement would then receive the same amount of water. Any water that leeched into the soil while it was running through the canals would come out in springs farther down the valley.[57] The proposal was significant, considering the investment that the Saints already had in the existing canal network.

TABLE 2.1
Irrigation canals on the Muddy

Number of canals	Place	Length (miles)	Average width (feet)	Average depth (feet)	Cost	Acres of useful land
10	Lower Muddy	52.5	5.7	2	$62,320	6,230
4	Upper Muddy	13	5.2	1.9	$18,520	1,700
TOTAL 14		65.5			$80,840	7,930

SOURCE: Bleak, Annals, December 31, 1869.
NOTE: The chart is extracted from a report on irrigation for every settlement in the Southern Utah Mission.

In the St. Thomas area, the Saints had already built more than fifty miles of ditches spread out over ten canals. These canals represented a tremendous investment in time and resources. If the water were to come from farther up the valley, the existing network of canals required reconfiguring to tie into the new source of water, a prospect that must have seemed daunting. They did not shrink from the work, though. When the Saints left the valley, there was a nine-mile canal down one side of the river, and they had plans to dig a canal on the other side.[58]

Water was definitely an essential part of agriculture on the Muddy. Another was hard labor. William Wood recorded in his journal the type of work necessary for farming on the Muddy. Upon arrival, he was assigned two and a half acres of swampy and wet land for hay. He also received five acres of upland that was covered with mesquite brush that had "thorns . . . strong enough to pierce a hole through a leather strap." Although the brush was not terribly tall, he was forced to dig as deep as five feet into the ground to clear the stumps. With the help of a hired Paiute, he created a pile of firewood that made "the best fire [he] ever burned."

The hard labor did not end with preparing the land for farming. He planted two and a half acres of cotton, from which he gathered a few bales. His hay land was so badly inundated that he had to cut a small quantity with his scythe, rake it up, and carry it to higher ground to be spread out and dried. To accomplish this, he had to bind it in a rope and carry it out on his back. After it dried, he had to rake it again and pile it to be ready to feed his stock. To get enough food to survive, he cradled the grain of other settlers at the rate of one bushel per acre.[59]

Producing enough food to survive was very important, but the main agricultural pursuit of the residents of St. Thomas was to produce cotton for the rest of the Saints in Utah. Cotton production on the Muddy was not regular throughout the Muddy Mission's tenure. The first year, St. Thomas and its sister settlement produced 5,000 pounds of cotton. The next year with a larger population, Bleak reported only 3,000 pounds from thirteen and a half acres of cotton land. That makes an average of 222.2 pounds per acre. In comparison, R. M. Eglestead, in 1865, produced 600 pounds on three-quarters of an acre, nearly four times the next year's average. In 1867 output ranged from 300 pounds per acre to as high as 800 pounds. According to President Snow, the only thing that was preventing the production of up to 100,000 pounds of cotton on the Muddy was the fact that only about 30 of the 158 called to settle on the Muddy in October 1867 were actually in the area a year later. Part of why Brigham Young continued to call people to the area was because he believed it would end up being the granary of the South, if only the "brethren are permitted to dwell there in peace."[60]

In some ways, Brigham Young's belief seemed to be well founded. They had several good years of wheat crops. In 1869 early estimates projected a yield of approximately three thousand bushels of wheat. Other crops produced well also. Andrew Gibbons claimed one year to have seven cuttings of alfalfa. Each one of the cuttings was two feet high and in blossom.[61] As has been the case in so many other places in the West, water proved the limiting factor.

In 1869 the flow of the Muddy was very light. In June the Saints in St. Thomas were not too concerned, because they had just completed the ditch that bypassed the swamp north of town. Though they had "no concern of scarcity" a mere two months before, by August it was becoming clear that conditions were not good. James Leithead reported to James Bleak that because of the scarcity of water, there was very little cotton, cane, or corn.[62] There was wheat, however. The poor cotton crop was to hit the town very hard.

The economy of the Muddy focused almost exclusively on cotton production. Because the cotton was not sold on the open market, there was very little money in the settlements, beyond what was brought in by selling hay and salt down the river to miners in Eldorado Canyon, or even as far as Yuma. Because the area was so money poor, most nonbarter exchanges utilized "bishop's chips." Bishop's chips were octagonal pieces of lead stamped with various values. The ward bishop issued them at the town store, where they were legal tender.[63] The settlers' situation was made even more complicated by the fact that because the store was not bringing any specie in and nobody was growing anything in salable quantities other than cotton, it could not afford to stock many goods. Anywhere outside of Zion, store owners could take either cash or a wide variety of goods in trade and obtain their goods from whomever they wanted to, rather than only from those interested in Mormon self-sufficiency.

This situation made cotton very important to the economy of St. Thomas, since it provided almost the sole means of securing goods from outside the valley. A letter from James Leithead to James Bleak shows just how bad of a situation the Saints on the Muddy were in. He wrote:

> In a letter last week to President Snow I said something about our cotton. I wish now to say or rather propose to the Rio Virgin M. Co., that if they will furnish us . . . with goods such as we will select, or rather, such as we are really in need of, such as shoes, clothing, partly home made, shovels, spades, hoes, ploughs, and articles of this kind that we are destitute of, we will agree to deliver our cotton, some 20 to 25 thousand pounds, providing we get the goods at about the same rate we have purchased them from the Southern Utah Co-op. We will freight our goods down and deliver the cotton at the factory. I make this offer because we are destitute of such articles, and our cotton is our only dependence to get them. If the Rio Virgin Co. cannot accede to something of this kind, we must try to find another market. . . . We care less about the price, could we only obtain the articles needed. Many are nearly naked for clothing. We can sell nothing we have for money, and the cotton, what little there it, seems to be all our hope in that direction. . . . Please ascertain the Company's mind on this subject at as early a date as possible, and communicate to me.[64]

The co-op agreed to meet the demands of the people on the Muddy, as the factory in Washington, Utah, was always in need of cotton to keep its machinery going.

Although it lacked the same economic importance to St. Thomas, salt was a very important commodity for the settlers. The mine was five miles from the town, but all land-bound traffic heading to the mine went through St. Thomas. It was a very valuable commodity for culinary, livestock, and mining uses. Everyone had free access to the mine and extracted their own salt. One day the proximity to the mine created a stir when a camel walked into town. When the Paiutes saw it, some thought that the Great White Spirit had sent it to punish them, so they ran away, afraid. There was a "dromedary line" between Los Angeles and Fort Mojave because some freighters thought that the camels would be better than horses for freighting salt in the desert. The plan proved unworkable because the rocks cut the camels' feet and made them sore. Additionally, the sight of the camels made their horses hysterical. The failed business owners turned the camels loose in the desert to fend for themselves.[65]

Life in St. Thomas was not just about raising food, growing cotton, and mining salt. Residents were determined to create a real community with all the benefits that their previous homes had offered. An early effort to establish a school began in 1865. Students met in the home of Moses Gibson. Residents also held many social gatherings, seeming to look for any occasion to have a party. When Hannah Sharp and her husband arrived in St. Thomas, the town organized a dance to celebrate their arrival. The fiddler had only two strings for his instrument, but the enthusiasm of the dancers made up for the deficiencies of the music. Dust billowed up from the floor as dancers performed the quadrille or polka. Their efforts urged those who were not dancing to stand outside in order to be able to breathe. On the nights that there was no dancing, Sister Sharp reported that her tent was a social hot spot, where crowds would gather to tell stories, sing, and laugh. Evidently, the lightheartedness was a matter of consternation to some of the leaders of the church, who compared the actions of the residents of St. Thomas to those of the Israelites making the golden calf while Moses was up on the mountain.[66]

The smallness of the community and the fact that so many of the people called there were married made the social lives of singles a little more difficult. Delaun Cox's dating experience illustrates just how difficult it could be. His children recorded that when Delaun was about nineteen years old, the young Charlotte Kelsey, who had just recently turned thirteen, arrived on the Muddy. He was not impressed at first sight, thinking, "What a homely overgrown girl she is." Be that as it may, she was instantly popular and spent the evening strolling with a man very much her senior. Humiliated by the wagging tongues brought about by a girl so young being out all evening with a much older man, she returned home to Washington County. Cox later traveled to Washington County on some business and meeting her there was astonished at how quickly beauty took the place of homeliness. Before he knew it, he was asking her if he could accompany her home.[67]

Despite the efforts of many to create a working community, there were, of course, those who were dissatisfied with the place. In March 1866, Betsy

Simons recorded in her journal that "if I were not here by council, I would not stay here any longer." Her faith in the divine approval of her call to the Muddy was the only thing that kept her there. Still others survived by simply leaving when the weather became unbearable and returning when it cooled. Erastus Snow lamented that so many St. Thomas residents summered in the North. He said that those who had genuine health concerns should, of course, absent themselves from the Muddy in the summer, or move entirely. However, "those who have not such a good excuse should put their shoulder to the wheel with their brethren and help to roll on the good work that has been so well begun in developing the resources of that region."[68]

Many who did stay year-round seemed to mirror the sentiments of Betsy Simons. When visiting St. Thomas in January 1867, Bleak found residents to be "highly discouraged." In a Sunday meeting, Bleak observed, "it seemed rather hard to get enough spirit in the people to have a meeting at all. [The] [o]fficers and people were apathetic."[69] Given their problems with their Paiute neighbors and with agriculture, it is understandable that some felt discouraged. Residents were also experiencing extreme difficulties with the state of Nevada over state boundaries and taxes. Despite this, many remained optimistic and faithful, though events to come would dampen that spirit.

In 1870 James Leithead received word that Brigham Young wanted to come inspect the settlements on the Muddy. Leithead had replaced Smith as bishop in St. Thomas in December 1867 when the former bishop's health had begun to fail. Young told Leithead that he wanted to do some exploring in Arizona, so he required a flat boat capable of carrying a wagon and team. Leithead sent teams to Sheep Mountain, sixty miles away, with no water on the way, to retrieve timber. Leithead and R. Broadbent erected a saw pit in a cottonwood grove to cut the planks they needed. They assembled, caulked, pitched, and launched the boat in preparation for the impending visit. President Young, however, was so disappointed in what he saw that he did not feel like exploring, and the effort was wasted. President Young, though disappointed with the area, told people to remain there, work, and act as if they were to remain forever. Some agreed with Young's negative assessment of the land and left the area against his counsel. Others were determined to make it work no matter the cost, some going so far as to purchase additional lands.[70] Unfortunately, such purchases proved to be misguided.

3

Now That We Are Here, Where Are We?

Boundary Disputes and the Abandoning of St. Thomas

In 1870 a federal survey showed that St. Thomas was in Nevada. Rather than submit to the state's high rate of taxation, the Saints voted to abandon the settlement after receiving permission from Brigham Young to do so if they so desired. The timing of the decision to leave was particularly poor for Israel Hoyt. Israel was in the mountains sawing lumber for a new home when the Saints received the letter from Brigham Young advising them to gather to discuss the fate of the mission. Arriving late on a Saturday night, he left the wagon loaded. At their worship service the next day, the missionaries received a release and advice to move elsewhere. Israel came home from the meeting, and when his wife expressed the need for wood for cooking, he threw down some of the lumber he had so arduously obtained and began chopping it up for firewood. His children stood around big-eyed and frightened, wondering if their father had lost his mind as he prepared for a very expensive cooking fire.[1] Though not everyone responded as dramatically as Brother Hoyt, this chapter recounts what must have been a very emotional time for the Saints on the Muddy.

When the Mormons established St. Thomas, nobody was entirely certain what state or territory it belonged to. The Mormons were content with a purely theocratic government. As this chapter shows, Arizona, Nevada, and Utah were not content to leave Caesar out of the picture. Government surveys finally located St. Thomas firmly in Nevada. After protracted legal wrangling, the Saints finally abandoned the Muddy Mission en masse, leaving only one dissenting family behind.

St. Thomas may have been remote from the main body of the Saints along the Wasatch Front and in Dixie, but they discovered that they were anything but remote when it came to interactions with the federal and state governments.[2] State boundary maneuvering between Arizona, Nevada, and Utah placed the town, at various times, in each state. This wrangling over jurisdiction proved to be the undoing of St. Thomas as part of the Muddy Mission and Utah community of Saints.

When the Saints first arrived in St. Thomas, they were much more concerned with building homes, digging ditches, and growing crops than in forming any local government. All secular decisions devolved to church leaders. This did not stop the three nearby states from attempting to bring the town into their respective political orbits. Thomas Smith reported to Salt Lake that in August 1865, officials from Fort Mojave in Arizona Territory visited St. Thomas and St. Joseph. These officials informed residents of the upcoming election the next month and informed Smith of his appointment as assessor and collector. They further informed residents of the impending division of Mojave County, and of the desire of residents at El Dorado to have a representative in the Arizona legislature from St. Thomas. The new county, Pah-Ute County, established their county seat at Callville.[3]

According to James Bleak, Elder Smith and his fellow missionaries "did not appear to be dazzled by the specious promises made by the visitors." In a letter to Erastus Snow, he indicated that they would not organize any precincts or hold any elections. Residents arrived at that decision after a council decided that elections would tend to "raise excitement and jealousy [and] would do us as a people more harm than good." This was not just a local decision. Apparently, the council simply ratified the advice given to Smith from Brigham Young, who counseled them to "let pollytics alone . . . we thought that to be nutral would be the best pollacy for us at present [sic]."[4]

The Saints in St. Thomas wished to retain their theocratic government. Bleak reported that the stake high council at St. George established the St. Thomas Ward on August 12, 1865. The ward was composed of missionaries in St. Thomas, St. Joseph, and Callville. The stake named Thomas Smith acting bishop of the ward. Confirming the Saints' dismissal of Arizona's overture, Bleak's entry for September 5, 1865, the day of the election in Arizona, affirmed again that no election occurred on the Muddy. Little did the Saints realize that in the same month in the nearby Pahranagat Valley, a miner

working in the new Pahranagat district wrote the governor of Nevada, asking for instructions on how to form a county.[5]

One way to illustrate the confusion over exactly what state St. Thomas
was in is to look at the establishment of post offices in towns on the Muddy.
When established, government records place the post office in St. Thomas
in Utah, in Washington County. A short time later, jurisdiction over the
area transferred to Pah-Ute County, Arizona. Also in 1866, the Nevada legislature created Lincoln County by splitting Nye County. Hiko claimed the
county seat, that town being the principal town in the Pahranagat Mining
District. In 1869 Utah tried to reclaim the area by forming Rio Virgin County,
which included all the Muddy settlements. The federal government declared
the area part of Nevada on January 18, 1867. Because no reliable survey
existed, neither Utah, Arizona, or Nevada officials nor Muddy Mission residents were absolutely sure what jurisdiction the valley lay in. The matter
remained unresolved until late 1870.

Lincoln County officials pined for taxable income from St. Thomas and
the other settlements on the Muddy. George Ernst, Lincoln County assessor,
identified in his 1868 report that the only taxable properties in the county
were in the Pahranagat Mining District, hardly enough to run such a large
jurisdiction. Add the Mormon settlements, he claimed, and the tax rolls doubled. When he tried to assess the Mormon properties, however, he had to
retreat because of the open hostility he faced.[6]

Ernst was not without allies. Nevada congressman Delos Ashley lobbied
heavily in the US House of Representatives to have the eastern border of
Nevada established along its current boundary. He argued that the people
in Pioche were a mining people and as such belonged not in pastoral Utah,
but in Nevada. He then said that Nevada's population of nearly fifty thousand annually paid three hundred thousand dollars in taxes to the federal

TABLE 3.1
Post offices on the Muddy

Town	County	Establishment date
St. Thomas	Washington County, Utah	July 23, 1866
St. Joseph	Pah-Ute County, Arizona	August 26, 1867
West Point	Rio Virgin County, Utah	September 20, 1869
Overton	Pah-Ute County, Arizona	April 25, 1870

SOURCE: "Record of Appointment of Postmasters, 1832–September 30, 1971," Publication
M841, Post Office Department Rg 28, UNLV Microforums HE6376.A1 N33X 1982a or UNLV Lied
Library.

government, whereas Utah's larger population paid only forty-one thousand dollars, and then most of it was paid in produce, not specie. "Let members [of Congress] decide," argued Ashley, "which is the most benefit to the United States." Given that the country was deeply indebted in the wake of the Civil War, Ashley's call found willing listeners. He did not, it is important to note, claim that the residents of the disputed area desired to live in Nevada.[7]

In the midst of this, Arizona again attempted to claim St. Thomas. On October 1, 1867, it moved the seat of Pah-Ute County from Callville to St. Thomas. This time the Saints did not rebuff the attempt. Octavius Gass of Callville and Andrew S. Gibbons of St. Thomas departed shortly thereafter to represent residents at the territorial legislature, held in Tucson beginning December 10, 1868. They started down the Colorado on November 1 in a boat built by James Leithead, but the trip did not go as planned.

The passage through Black Canyon, the site of Hoover Dam, prompted Gass to sit in the back of the boat gripping the sides and yell, "For God's sake, Andy, keep her pointed down stream." Fearful of attack by Native Americans, they kept the boat in the middle of the river, camping only in secluded areas. After they reached Fort Yuma, they had difficulty finding transportation since they arrived at about the same time as the news of a coach that had been waylaid and the driver killed. Consequently, they took their seats in the territorial assembly six days late.

Although Gass and Gibbons were not there when it passed, the Arizona legislature passed a memorial to send to Congress asking them to reconsider giving the Muddy to Nevada. They said, "It is the unanimous wish of the inhabitants . . . that the territory in question should remain with Arizona; for the convenient transaction of official and other business, and on every account they greatly desire it." One St. Thomas resident was very skeptical of the efficacy of the legislature effort. Writing about Andrew Gibbons's return to St. Thomas in his journal, Darius Clement penned, "They doubtless labored with commendable zeal, but very little benefit accrued to their constituents through their services."[8]

Utah was not content to concede the area to Nevada, either. On February 18, 1869, in Salt Lake City, the Utah legislature created Rio Virgin County out of Washington County. The legislature designated St. Joseph as the county seat. Church leadership did not explicitly approve the action. Nevertheless, Brigham Young's nephew and apostle Joseph W. Young received an appointment to be the first probate judge of the new county. As an apostle, he would have never accepted the appointment if it ran counter to the wishes of the president and remain in his position. Joseph W. Young held his first county court on April 3, 1869, at St. Joseph.[9]

Nevada did not remain quiescent while Utah and Arizona were maneuvering. In July 1869, Lincoln County officials sent a man whom the sources identify only as "Carlow" to attempt once more the assessing of the settlements on the Muddy. Residents recognized him and ran him out of town. Muddy Mission residents doubly reviled him because he was an apostate Mormon and arrived on July 24, Pioneer Day, when he felt that the missionaries would be too distracted by their celebrations. In 1870 the Lincoln County assessor and surveyor said, "I found it very difficult to make an assessment at all, and utterly out of my power to collect; yet with constant protests, and many threats, I managed to make an assessment." He finally determined that the taxes due Nevada in that part of the state amounted to $61,700, but if "the question of Jurisdiction be finally settled, and a correct assessment made, it would greatly exceed that amount."[10] The amount was for all the settlements on the Muddy, not just St. Thomas.

In 1870 Lincoln County stepped up its efforts to bring St. Thomas and the other Muddy settlements under its de facto jurisdiction. When the Lincoln County sheriff served summons to the Saints at Meadow Valley, the First Presidency in Salt Lake advised them to show their receipts for taxes paid in Utah, advice repeated elsewhere for those on the Muddy. Church leaders reasoned that the Saints would be subject to the laws of Nevada once the boundary line was officially drawn. President Young advised the Saints to arm themselves and defend their property, even by force if required. The Saints, if they needed any further motivation to resist, found it in the form of the prosecuting attorney for the county. He was also an apostate Mormon who had been prominent in the early church but had become a reorganite.[11] Those defending their property understood that they would receive no quarter from the county.

Because of the very real threat of violence over the issue, Erastus Snow sought to intercede with Nevada officials. Bleak copied a letter that Snow wrote to Bishop Henrie of Panaca, stating:

> Since writing to you and Bishop Hatch by last mail, I have had another talk with the Acting Governor, who advised the U.S. Supreme Court for the Territory of Utah to issue an injunction against the Sheriff of Lincoln County, Nevada, or any

of his deputies or assistants, restraining them from any attempt at collecting taxes until the line is officially determined; and told men that the Court was willing to issue such a writ, and place it in the hands of a Deputy Marshal, or a Special Deputy among you, ready to serve whenever attempts shall be made to collect. I have requested the attorney general to have such an injunction issued ready to forward to you by next mail. . . . I think this will be a better course. Try to keep down any violent measures until it be definitely known. You had better send an agent to answer for you at the Hiko Court so as to avoid, if possible, any further excitement, or great expense or more angry feeling, in case you should find yourselves in Nevada.[12]

Because Snow was the president of the Southern Utah Mission, he spoke for residents of St. Thomas as well on this issue.

St. Thomas residents did not object to being residents of Nevada out of principle. Taxation was the biggest issue. The treasurer's report of June 6, 1870, for Rio Virgin County shows just how little in taxes missionaries on the Muddy paid. Officials transferred $24.00 from Pah-Ute County, Arizona, coffers, which gave the total contents of the treasury $180.19. The treasurer paid $119.00 in county warrants and had $28.55 in cash, $20.00 in flour, $12.45 in wheat, and an underbalance of $0.19, making a total of $180.19.[13] Up until 1870, residents paid taxes to both Utah and Arizona. Nevada had attempted to tax St. Thomas in 1867, 1868, and 1869. If those efforts had been successful, residents would have seen their tax rates tripled.

Nevada had some of the highest taxes in the United States at the time. In Rio Virgin County, Utah, in 1870, officials raised taxes from one-half mil to three-quarters mil. Nevada, on the other hand, required 3 percent state and county tax, stamp tax, license tax, and poll tax. Residents would not have simply paid a third more than they had already paid. In Utah they could pay their taxes in kind. The requirement that Nevada taxes were payable only in gold and silver coin was especially onerous to the agriculturally oriented Saints. Because gold and silver were scarce in Mormon communities, it was more valuable than in areas where it was more readily available. This had the net effect of raising taxes even higher. Even had the Saints been inclined to pay the higher taxes, they had little faith the tax money would be used responsibly. In a letter to Congress on behalf of the Saints on the Muddy, apostle George A. Smith wrote, "The cession of these settlements to Nevada may seem a small matter, but that state is the heaviest taxed in the union, and ignores the federal currency, its taxes must be paid in gold; it[s] counties are also deeply in debt. Most of its officials are mere adventurers, who wish to raise the wind somehow and go to a better country."[14]

Available records show that the Saints on the Muddy felt that they were being treated unfairly by Lincoln County officials. Although there may have some anti-Mormon attitudes held by those officials, they were attempting to carry out their legal responsibilities. They had no doubt that the Muddy was in Nevada, and as Nevada residents, the missionaries needed to be subject to taxation just like any other resident of the state. Whereas the Saints may have found it difficult to pay their taxes in specie, other Nevada residents managed to comply with the requirement. It was not the fault of Lincoln County officials that the Saints had not paid their Nevada taxes since 1866 or that they had paid them to the wrong governmental agency, namely, the territory of Utah. Because of the injustices that the Mormons as a group had experienced previously, the Saints on the Muddy may have been predisposed to feel as if they were being treated unfairly because of their religion rather than their lack of fiscal responsibility.

Knowing that a survey was being conducted that would make a final determination as to which state their settlement was in, residents of St. Thomas spent the last months of 1870 in anxiety. James Leithead reported to Erastus Snow that in all the settlements on the Muddy, he had found uncertainty and doubt about the permanence of the Muddy Mission. Brigham Young's recent visit did little to assuage this sentiment, nor did the breaking up of the settlements on the Upper Muddy. There were, however, many who did wish to stay. They "feel as though it would be hard after so many years of toil, to abandon . . . what little progress they have made towards a home. I have tried to encourage the Saints, those who feel this way, to persevere."[15]

There were those who did not choose to persevere as President Snow desired, feeling that the writing was on the wall. Ruth Cornia recalled her early departure from the Muddy while her children were sick with cholera. "My, we had a time eating chickens. We couldn't sell them or anything so what we couldn't take with us we had to leave for the Indians. We weren't out of sight of our home before the Indians had set fire to it. We left December 3 and went to Pine Valley where we stayed with my Aunt Sophia M. Burgess."[16]

On December 19, 1870, Bleak recorded that the boundary survey had been completed and that all the settlements on the Muddy were officially in Nevada. Brigham Young, George A. Smith, and Erastus Snow wrote to James

Leithead and the Saints on the Muddy with instructions on how to proceed. They advised that despite the positives the location had, their isolation from market and high taxes may make staying untenable. They advised the calling of a general meeting and a vote to remain or leave, but that all should abide by the will of the majority. They also advised the settlers to petition Congress and the Nevada Assembly for relief from their burden of taxation.[17] In order to comply with the wishes of Brigham Young and chart a new course for the Muddy Saints, residents held a meeting in St. Thomas on December 20. In that meeting, they voted to abandon the Muddy. The group appointed a delegation to go look for a new place to settle. The records of the Moapa Stake report that in the vote to abandon the Muddy, 63 elected to leave. Only 2 voted to stay, Daniel and Ann Bonelli. The meeting in St. Thomas must have almost depopulated the rest of the Muddy Mission, since the 1870 census listed only about 150 people.[18]

Daniel Bonelli was born in Switzerland in 1836. He joined the church as a young man. He served as a missionary in his native land, baptizing more than 300 people. Bonelli came to America in 1859. While crossing the Atlantic, he met Ann Haigh from England, whom he married shortly after landing in the States. He was a very intelligent man—he reportedly spoke six languages. The decision of the Bonellis to remain in St. Thomas did not derive from sheer stubbornness. According to Warren Foote, the Bonellis were in a state of apostasy, being believers in "the New Movement."[19]

The New Movement was officially launched in October 1869 by William S. Godbe and associates. Godbe was one the ten wealthiest men in the Utah Territory and a disaffected member of the church. The Godbeites started a spiritualist movement, a "Church of Zion" nominally headed by Amasa Lyman, an apostle who had been disfellowshipped.[20] The main thrust of their argument was that Brigham Young's economic policies were wrong and that the Saints should assimilate economically with the East. Their church quickly foundered, and the movement quietly dropped its religious bent to focus on social reforms, claiming that the LDS Church should confine itself to spiritual affairs. Bonelli's acceptance of the Godbeite doctrine explains his refusal to abandon his investment in southern Nevada.

After the meeting, residents immediately began preparing to move. Warren Foote's mill ran constantly so the Saints could move their flour to St. George. He did not finish grinding until February 16, at which time he disassembled the mill and moved it to Utah. In order to have enough wagons and teams to evacuate the Saints, Brigham Young called on people in St. George to help. Many answered that call. According to the records of the Moapa Stake, "The people generally looked upon the vacating of their homes and the labor of years thrown away joyfully, and rejoiced in the providence of God."[21] It is hard to imagine that this was truly the case, but at least the newly dispossessed must have put on a happy face about the situation.

Because the Saints felt it was imperative to leave quickly to avoid prosecution by county officials, they were not able to take everything they might have otherwise. Parts of the mill were not portable. All the lumber in their houses that had to be hauled great distances over poor roads remained behind. Much of the livestock had to be either slaughtered and quickly eaten or left and retrieved later. The biggest nonportable investment was the miles of canals along the Muddy, a system that they told Congress cost them one hundred thousand dollars to construct.

While the Saints prepared to leave, church leaders in Salt Lake arranged for a place for them to resettle in Utah. In a letter of January 24, 1871, to H. S. Eldridge, Daniel H. Wells spoke of their destination. He wrote that settlers from the Muddy and Meadow Valley area were anxious to leave because of the high taxes and unfriendly neighbors. "This move will greatly help the settlements of the new 'Land of Canaan'; as many of those leaving the Nevada settlements will locate at Kanab and in the surrounding regions." Brigham Young sent letters to the Saints who left Long Valley, which is north of Kanab, in the face of Native American hostilities in 1866. He asked them to relinquish their claims to the area so the Saints from Nevada would have a place to go. For those unwilling to relinquish their claims, he asked them to state their terms. Erastus Snow encouraged those who felt that they must be paid to be generous in their terms to the displaced. President Young also instructed the bishops in Long Valley to treat sales of land to anyone besides those from the Muddy as null and void.[22]

The main body of residents left on February 1, 1871. The long lines of wagons leaving the Muddy Valley reminded some observers of the camps of Israel that followed Moses out of Egypt. The roads leaving the valley were no better than they were when the Saints were arriving, with more than thirty crossings of the Virgin River. The evacuees also found it necessary to break trail through snow in the Santa Cruz Mountains, which, Samuel Claridge said, "made it very uncomfortable." As they left, some residents realized that they would never return, so they destroyed their property rather than see it fall into the hands of those who drove them out. John Kartchner set his house on fire as they rolled away rather than leave it to the Paiutes.[23]

It was a very unpleasant day for those staying behind as well. It was raining, and Ann Bonelli was having a baby. As the teams rolled out, a few sisters stayed until the last wagon to deliver the baby. The sisters then got on the wagon and left, leaving the newly increased Bonelli family alone in the rain. Daniel Bonelli would later say that he did not so much leave the church as it abandoned him.[24]

On February 8, the Lincoln County sheriff arrived from Hiko to serve summons to all the brethren still on the Muddy. Finding the people were leaving the state, the sheriff declared his intention to return and make oath of the facts, get attachments on personal property, and return with sufficient posse to enforce the writ. Following the sheriff's visit, residents held a meeting in which the remaining Saints determined to leave en masse by March 1 in order to avoid having their teams and wagons confiscated. All the loose stock had already been taken out by Price W. Nelson. Any inclined to linger were hurried along by the fact that the total amount of tax and cost for 1870 alone would have been about twelve thousand dollars in gold coin. As the Saints left, there were miners and other opportunists that flocked to the valley to take up the land and improvements left by the departing Saints.[25]

The time of St. Thomas as the main settlement in the Muddy Mission was over. The seeming rapacity of Nevada officials was not the only factor that caused the settlement to fail. Excluding matters of faith, Bonelli's adherence to the New Movement made economic sense. Tax rates in the Silver State were very high, but there were resources in the area that would have allowed the Saints to survive. The missionaries on the Muddy were unable to identify a strong market community because of the church's insistence that they participate in the cotton experiment of the Southern Utah Mission. That lack of diversification prevented them from developing a more secure economic base.[26] Economics, politics, and environment do not reveal the full story of the first seven years of St. Thomas and the Muddy Mission. Active members of the church pointed to a belief that God blesses those who sacrifice in his name. Because of their obedience in settling and building up St. Thomas, the Saints were laying up treasures in heaven, the only place where treasure truly mattered to them. Regardless of outlook, what is certain is that one chapter in the life of the town had definitely ended.

4

"Not a Town of the Past . . ."
From Zion to the Silver State

After the Mormon exodus, St. Thomas was a much different place. Opportunists moved in and stripped the town of everything of value. For a time, the town looked more like Dodge City than Salt Lake City, with prospecting, hard drinking, gambling, and horse racing. The experience of the Syphus family shows just how different a town St. Thomas was after the Saints left. Luke and Julie Syphus moved to St. Thomas in 1887, as Luke had received the contract to carry the mail to area mining camps. His duties required him to be gone every other night. To protect his wife, Syphus built a platform high up in a cottonwood tree where she kept her bed. On the nights he was away, Julie climbed up her perch and drew the ladder up behind her. She would then lay trembling with fear, "as the drunken desperadoes rode the streets shooting their guns and yelling out foul language."[1]

It is not just polite white society that fell apart. Changes in policies toward the Paiutes brought deterioration in white-Native American relationships as well as the creation of the Moapa Paiute Reservation. The general lawlessness did not prevail indefinitely, however. Toward the end of the nineteenth century, Mormons returned to the Moapa Valley, where they established a school, reestablished the St. Thomas Ward, and generally put the town on a more stable economic footing.

The departing missionaries sent a party of nine explorers to reconnoiter the area in Kane County, arriving on Christmas Day, 1870. The explorers found a valley one hundred yards wide to three-quarters of a mile wide and barely twenty miles long. The east fork of the Virgin River ran the length of the valley, but it scarcely held enough water to irrigate the thirteen hundred acres of arable land. Abraham Kimball, speaking of the valley, said, "Of all the vallies [*sic*] I ever saw it was one, no one team could pull an empty wagon out of it [because of its high sides], and hardly wide enough to turn a wagon around."[2]

The church also faced the unresolved issue of obtaining cotton. A main priority for the settlement of Utah's Dixie was for the production of cotton, and from 1865 to 1870 the Muddy Mission provided most of the cotton that came out of the area. Erastus Snow sent letters to the settlers who remained, asking them to place a renewed emphasis on cotton growing to compensate for the lost production.[3]

The missionaries on the Muddy barely made a clean getaway from Nevada. Besides their difficulties with state and county officials, the Saints faced other difficulties as they fled. Brigham Young described the exodus thus: "As the brethren left their homes . . . there were stragglers hanging around like sharks in the wake of a ship—who slipped into the houses of the saints so soon as they left them and commenced gathering up every thing of value and taking possession of the best houses &c. . . . [T]he Indians set fire to the houses as soon as the Saints left, and before the latter were out of sight nothing remained of their pleasant homes but the blackened walls." This move, caused by the "rapacity and hostility of the political cormorants who devour the earnings of the people of Nevada," was made even more miserable by the almost two feet of snow that fell in the Beaver Dam area during their exodus.[4]

Arriving in Long Valley on the first of March, the missionaries quickly planted spring wheat and established a town they named Glendale. Continuing their streak of bad luck, the new transplants saw grasshoppers destroy their crops.[5] A smaller number of the displaced Saints settled in Orderville, four miles to the south. Others simply went back to the places they had been called from in the first place.

The Mormons' time on the Muddy left a complicated legacy. William Wood, who had given up a successful business and a comfortable brick home in Salt Lake City when called in 1867, ended up back in Salt Lake living in a dugout. When he asked his wife, Elizabeth, if she would rather they had never left in the first place, she replied, "I am glad you have filled your missions, and would rather be in this dugout with your mission filled, than in that fine house with your mission unfilled." Despite their poor condition upon their return to Salt Lake, Wood managed to reestablish himself, and when Elizabeth died in 1887, she was living comfortably. James H. Wood, a direct descendant, claimed that Elizabeth "often testified that Brigham Young's prophetic statement made to she and William and their three little boys on the road at Provo had been fulfilled—'You go and fill that mission and God will bless you!'"[6]

Elizabeth Wood's sentiments were not unusual given that she remained an active member of the church her whole life. Mormons were no strangers to sacrifice. Non-Mormons generally held a different view of the Muddy Mission. The editor of the *Salt Lake Tribune,* in particular, was critical of the decision of the missionaries to abandon their settlements. He wrote, "It is presumable that the Spirit of Revelation knew where the boundaries of Utah Territory were, and it is also supposable that knowing all things, it should have been acquainted with what the Nevadans would do if the church located . . . settlements upon their territory." He was very critical that settlers were given the choice of throwing away years of labor and leaving or staying and being considered apostates "to remain with their little all." In all fairness, the reader should understand that the church did very little of which the editor of the *Salt Lake Tribune* was not critical. For those not of the faith, the decision to leave seemed to be sheer folly. Later settlers were able to survive because they did not grow cotton and were able to have economic dealings with non-Mormons.[7]

The determination to cut their losses and relocate left the Saints with very little bargaining power when they tried to liquidate their few possessions. Nevertheless, some tried to dispose of what property they could. Before leaving, they negotiated with a Gentile named Isaac Jennings to buy cows and property. All they received from Jennings and his associates was a promise to pay once he harvested the crops, and then only one and a half cents per pound, which would cover only the cost of the seed. The wheat crop was good that year, and Jennings reportedly harvested eight thousand bushels, for which he received six cents a pound. He also tore down houses to sell the lumber for ten cents a board foot. One source reported that Jennings tore down several buildings because he heard a rumor that some of the newly departed were considering returning to the area. He dismantled and sold the lumber to forestall their return. He had a ready market for his agricultural goods, selling grain to the Paiute Agency. He was also able to utilize cheap Paiute labor to grow his crops. Despite all this, the *Deseret News* reported in 1875 that Jennings lost all his money and left the area a broken man. Not everyone who left was involved with the agreement with Jennings. Warren Foote said that he "would rather have given his to the Indians than these fellows to speculate on."[8] The Saints never received the money promised them by Jennings.

Mormons are strongly encouraged by their leaders to be a record-keeping people. The settlers who took their place in St. Thomas after the exodus were not similarly motivated, as evidenced by the paucity of available historical accounts covering the entire 1870s. One observer described the town during this period as the epitome of the western frontier. The town became a rendezvous for outlaws, cattle rustlers, and horse thieves because of its isolation and available water and forage. The most notorious of these outlaws were Jack Reed, nicknamed "Black Jack"; Shan Balden; and a man by the name of Siebrecht. Not everyone who settled in St. Thomas was an outlaw, though nearly all were single men. Some just wanted to live life undisturbed by the confines of regulated society. The presence of miners and Native Americans along with outlaws completed a trifecta of quintessential characters of the mythic West.

Regardless of anyone's motivations for taking up residence in the area, most of the land reverted to the desert, as the fields, orchards, and vineyards deteriorated. The January 26, 1875, edition of the *Deseret News* carried the report of a traveler who had recently visited St. Thomas. He claimed that the "once lively Mormon settlement has now a peculiarly desolate appearance which brings vividly to mind Oliver Goldsmith's masterly production of the 'Deserted Village.'"[9]

The establishment of the Muddy Mission was a conscious attempt to expand the borders of Zion, to create sacred space. Those replacing the Saints on the Muddy may have not consciously been thwarting the interests of the LDS Church, but their control of the land was a direct attack on the land's sacredness. Some of these new residents lived their lives about as far away from the patterns pursued by the Saints as possible, living on the edge of society and over the edge of the law. One of the most interesting new residents was Jack Reed.

Reed has a significant place in the lore of St. Thomas, and his story played out in numerous journals and remembrances. Ute Vorace Perkins recalled playing along a ditch and bending down for a drink. His friend stopped him, saying that he met Jack Reed there the summer before. Reed was living in a tent under a tree. He had terrible sores on his legs and would wash them in the ditch. Perkins reported that Reed ended up in St. Thomas under the care of Mrs. Jennings. One day Perkins's mother visited Mrs. Jennings and watched Reed have his dressings changed. Mrs. Perkins asked Reed if he felt he was improving. He replied, "No lady, I am getting no better, at times the pain eases a little but I will never get well and for a reason, lady, I was in the mob that killed the Mormon Prophet Joseph Smith in Carthage Jail and every man who was in the mob has suffered just such as I am suffering, by the flesh being eaten off their bones by worms." Mrs. Perkins reportedly saw the worms in his flesh and the oozing sores. When Reed died, residents rolled him in canvas and buried him in an unmarked grave.[10]

Reed had the reputation in some quarters as a Robin Hood figure, but not all the outlaws maintained such a positive reputation despite their troubles with the law, as the experience of the Syphus family shows. St. Thomas residents did not just have criminals to worry about, as whites and Paiutes alike caroused and raised havoc. The October 14, 1882, edition of the *Pioche Weekly Record* described the current situation in St. Thomas: "Everything is not jes zaclky as it wus when u hurd from thes quarters afore. We hav been mad down hear, and one Piute got stabed in the back, and several Lamenites had jes a little too much firewater fur thur good. An one Gentile wus mity mad, but he didn't hurt enybody by it. U understand now that Sant Tomas is not a town of the past any longer. No sur, she kumin to the frunt, she iz."[11]

Even if they were not total outlaws, some of those who settled at St. Thomas brought a checkered past with them. Andrew Jackson "Jack" Long-street's origins are unclear. He was born sometime around 1838, possibly in Louisiana. His most noticeable feature was the lack of one ear, a feature he kept hidden under long blond hair. In his youth, he belonged to a group of horse thieves. When his group was apprehended, the authorities hung the rest, but spared him because of his extreme youth and cut off his ear to teach him a lesson and warn others of his background. Despite this history, his biographer, Sally Zanjani, takes great pains to paint Longstreet as the quint-essential western gunfighter, but one who adhered to a strict moral code, showing himself to be well outside the criminal underclass. Essentially, everybody he killed richly deserved it, or at least that was the legend sur-rounding him.

Longstreet made his first historically verifiable appearance in the South-west in 1861 at Eldorado Canyon, on the Nevada side of the Colorado River.

Eldorado, besides being a mining camp, was also a haven for criminals and deserters from the Civil War. Longstreet ran a small store near one of the principal mines. His name appears on some mining claims in 1880 Arizona, and in 1882 he moved to St. Thomas, on the Muddy.[12]

Apparently deciding that it was more lucrative to sell goods to miners than mine himself, Longstreet opened a saloon and drugstore in St. Thomas, as it was a "grate stopin plac for the publick." It did not take long for the new business to have an impact on the town. A mere fifteen days after the business opened, one *Pioche Weekly Record* correspondent noted, "Mr. Jack Longstreet flung is dores open to the public on the 17th uv Sept., an we've had more fites since then enybody's town—it's the salun and drug store I speak uv."[13] While in St. Thomas, one of Longstreet's favorite pastimes was horse racing.

Native Americans, outlaws, and respectable whites alike in St. Thomas enjoyed horse racing. Massive sums were bet on races, and whenever one was held, most of the valley turned out to watch. "Tramp," a correspondent from the Muddy, recounted one notable race. Moapa Valley resident Pat Curlin sold his ranch and went horse racing. He bought a horse and bet twelve hundred dollars on a race against Longstreet's Indian pony. Curlin arranged for the "Chief of the Muddy Indians" to ride the horse in the race. The night before the race, the chief was "doped" and his drawers, nightcap, and nightshirt stolen. Curlin's trainer had to race the next day and narrowly lost.[14]

The race and the circumstances surrounding it were just the beginning of the problems between a man named Dry and Longstreet in regards to horses. About a year later, the two fought over the purchase of a horse that ended with Longstreet repossessing the animal. In May 1884, the duo, apparently having settled their differences, departed St. Thomas together, heading north. Sometime later, Longstreet returned and said that when he and Dry had reached the big bend of the Muddy between St. Thomas and the reservation, Dry turned his guns on him. Longstreet shot and killed Dry in self-defense. In the absence of any witnesses to the contrary, Longstreet was quickly acquitted by Justice Megarrigle of St. Thomas. Longstreet was also implicated in another killing in 1886, but was never charged. The victim in that crime was accused of irregularities in a deal regarding horses as well.[15]

The Mormons' departure from St. Thomas and the rest of the Muddy also drastically changed the dynamic between whites and the Paiutes. In June 1871, when Andrew Sproul and Woodruff Alexander went back to retrieve the remainder of their belongings, they found that those who had moved in were having trouble with their neighbors. Some of the Paiutes had drowned three cows in a spring, which led the settlers to attempt to "teach them a lesson." The only thing that saved the thirty whites from the three hundred armed Paiutes was the accidental discharge of a Henry repeating rifle that spooked the larger group.[16]

In 1869 the Bureau of Indian Affairs sent Reuben N. Fenton to serve as agent for the Paiutes on the Muddy, even though there was no reservation set aside for their exclusive use. Fenton's headquarters started out in St. Thomas, but then shifted to Hiko, and then to Pioche. At first his job was relatively easy, because as long as there were Mormons in St. Thomas and surrounding towns to "sho[o]t them with biscuits," relations with the Paiutes remained workable.[17] Once the Mormons were gone, there was no buffer between the Moapa Paiutes and other whites, whites who were not nearly as willing to give food to their Native neighbors.

The Paiutes' food situation was already precarious when the Saints were preparing to leave the Moapa Valley. Captain Fenton wrote to the commissioner of Indian affairs in Washington, DC, requesting funds to purchase for the Paiutes some beef, flour, and other necessities. Apparently, the Mojaves had driven the Paiutes into the white settlements, and the starving tribe was killing stock, stealing grain, and being a "general annoyance."[18] The situation for the Paiutes deteriorated further when the Saints left the valley, taking all their livestock with them.

Fenton may have expressed concern for his charges, but in reality he did very little during his time as agent other than enrich himself at public expense. Bureau of Indian Affairs audits in June and September 1870 detailed some of the problems. One recorded that "no Report from Capt. Fenton of any visits to Indians have been received as yet at this office, and the voucher [requesting reimbursement] cannot therfor be verified as to the number of journeys, their extent or necessity." Fenton could not account for property purchased in behalf of the agency, and the amount requested for rental reimbursement seemed unnecessarily high. The auditor reported several other irregularities as well.[19]

On June 2, 1871, Fenton must have decided he could no longer get away gaming the system, so he attempted to leave town. The Lincoln County sheriff pursued and arrested him for attempting to skip out on the debts that he owed. Henry A. Fish, Fenton's clerk, sent an explanatory letter to Bureau of

Indian Affairs headquarters, laying out the many ways Fenton abused his position. Fish claimed that Fenton filed spurious travel papers and received reimbursement for supposed escort services. According to Fish, Fenton made no trips in the service of the Indian department. Despite vouchers and invoices to the contrary, Fish reported that "no beef cattle has ever been furnished these Indians. . . . [He] has never rented any office in Pioche or purchased any fuel for office purposes or any other purpose, no medicine has ever been issued . . . to these Indians except on one occasion." For that one occasion, Fenton charged ten dollars to his personal account at the drugstore. That account remained unpaid when Fenton tried to skip town. To back up his assertions, Fish included a list of charged and actual costs for the second and third quarters of 1870.[20]

To replace Fenton, and on the recommendation of the Baptists' national association, the commissioner sent Henry G. Stewart. Stewart arrived in Pioche only to discover that Fenton had made off with or destroyed all the agency's papers, and not only were there no funds, but it was all but guaranteed that nobody in town would extend any more credit to the agency. In poor health when he arrived, Stewart died in July 1871. The commissioner replaced him with Charles F. Powell, who had previously served as agent at the Fort Hall Reservation in Idaho.

Shortly after Powell arrived in Pioche, he was visited by two large groups of Paiutes. They were in very rough shape, naked and nearly starved. He used the scant resources available to feed and clothe them. Powell recognized that it was the departure of the Mormons that had made their situation so dire, writing that the Mormon "removal and the necessary farming has left the Indians in fact nothing to subsist upon and unless provided for, must either steal or starve." The solution was very clear for Powell, who wrote to his superiors, "I cannot too earnestly recommend the establishment of a Reservation for these Indians on the Muddy at St. Thomas."[21]

Powell would not see the reservation created while he was agent. He was replaced in 1872 by George W. Ingalls, who was retained as agent when President Ulysses Grant issued an executive order creating a thirty-nine-hundred-square-mile reservation for the Paiutes. The next year, Congress expanded it even more to include timber and additional farmland, creating the Southwest Nevada Indian Agency in 1873, headquartered in St. Thomas. The reservation was two million acres, or thirty-nine thousand square miles. It was the administrative center for thirty-one tribes from Utah,

Arizona, Nevada, and California. Ingalls used his position to convince six of the tribes to take up farming along the Muddy. Ingalls felt that conditions along the Muddy were ideal for "civilizing" the Paiutes by making them farmers because of the existing seventy-five-thousand-dollar irrigation system that was free to the government. This is ironic, considering that one justification for taking the land from Utah and giving it to Nevada was that the land was best suited for a mining people.[22]

Agency headquarters did not remain in St. Thomas for long, as Ingalls found himself infected with the mining bug and moved agency headquarters back to Pioche. This afforded him easy access to mining opportunities, but isolated him from his charges. Travelers passing through the area complained of harassment by Paiutes who demanded to know where the agent was. According to one reporter, they "never knew their agent and were given only the most putrid portions of flabby and stinking salt pork."[23]

White settlers on the Muddy grew very frustrated with the incompetence and corruption of the agents. Daniel Bonelli wrote to the commissioner to complain, saying that while the agents have "strutted about the streets of some far off mining town" wasting up to 90 percent of the reservation's funds on alcohol, gambling, and "den[s] of infamy," the Indians were left to beg and steal. Farmers were compelled to "buy peace" with more than a quarter of their entire food production. Congress had made appropriations sufficient to meet the needs of the Paiutes and protect settlers and travelers, but the "settler has suffered inconceivable annoyance . . . [and] perpetual anxiety, the Indians have gone naked, hungry and prowling and the traveler has fallen by their blows by the side of his desert pathway and the bones of scores of them are bleaching upon the desert plains."[24]

The Paiutes may not have written letters, but they did not take their treatment lying down. The *Tri-Weekly Ely Record* of September 11, 1872, related numerous instances when the Paiutes showed their unwillingness to tolerate their situation. A man named James was chased from his dwelling, was shot at, and had two fingers cut off with a shovel by some disgruntled Native Americans. Another man by the name of Stewart was forced to take refuge in his house when fired upon by some Paiutes. He was so shaken by the experience that he sold his property for a very low price and was glad to escape unscathed. The county assessor encountered some Paiutes who demanded he pay a toll for passage. He barely avoided paying it, "but it was a hard, close game." St. Thomas residents reported Paiutes running around the village in the middle of the night carrying torches. They claimed they were catching rabbits, but residents viewed it as a threat. Residents demanded that the Indian agent move his headquarters back to the Muddy and address the situation immediately, or trouble would ensue.[25]

There is very little in existing records to indicate that any agents ever heeded these warnings. There are some indications that agency officials actually made relationships between Paiutes and whites worse. On August 28, 1871, several Paiutes came to St. Thomas to return some horses that they had stolen. One, Ter-ra-Kuts, claimed Captain Fenton and William Patterson, a cattle buyer, instigated the thefts.[26] Given Fenton's track record, it may well have been true.

Beyond agency mismanagement, the simple creation of the reservation brought problems with whites as well. The *Pioche Daily Record* called the reservation an outrage. Those who squatted on the land after the Saints left suddenly found themselves on reservation land, for which the government offered the scant sum of thirty-two thousand dollars. Daniel Bonelli in particular lobbied against selling the land to the government under the terms offered. In a letter to the commissioner of Indian affairs, Bonelli very politely threatened the government with legal action and heavy lobbying of Congress if satisfactory compensation was not arranged. Even the agent, Ingalls, was not happy with the reservation. His objection was that the reservation was much larger than the Paiutes actually needed. He wrote his superiors, saying, "There is but a very small portion of this territory that is at all suitable for reservation purposes, and that portion is embraced in the valley of the Muddy."[27] Bonelli and others objected to the size of the reservation because it took in large amounts of land that could be valuable for mining and should not be off-limits to whites.

According to Bonelli, most of the farmers who were being displaced by the reservation did not object to selling out to the government as long as they were fairly compensated. Isaac Jennings and his wife, Grace, hatched a plan to detach St. Thomas from the reservation. Mrs. Jennings traveled to Washington, DC, to convince Congress to do just that. She claimed to represent all the white people in the Moapa Valley. Bonelli wrote to Edward Smith, Indian commissioner, refuting that assertion, claiming that there was no other person in the valley who agreed. He called it "a mere trap, an opening for friction, trouble, and expense and utterly infeasible," as no honest man would wish to live on the reservation or close to it. The only reason any were left was that they were waiting for their compensation from the government.[28]

Mrs. Jennings's visit to Congress frustrated the plans of those waiting for that compensation. While the legislators were deliberating on the bills that would have delivered the amounts appraised by Agents Powell and Ingalls, she arrived and convinced them that the settlers were not okay with the settlement. With the help of Joseph W. Young, all the canals, trees, houses, and the like owned by the Mormons but not claimed by settlers were donated to the government for the benefit of the Paiutes. The Paiutes did not get to enjoy the benefits for long, as the size of the reservation was reduced from two million acres to one thousand in 1875. Under the Carter administration, the reservation was expanded to nearly seventy-two thousand acres in 1980. Despite President Grant's intentions, whites retained the best lands and water rights. For the Paiutes, almost nothing remained.[29]

A letter from a concerned citizen in 1877 shows how bad the situation was for the Paiutes on the reservation. Robert Logan reported that the agency farm was a mass of weeds, and the whole operation was inexcusably ignored by the agent. The worst thing, according to Logan, was that the "poor Indians are dying of neglect." The agency had a large amount of medicine, yet the Paiutes were dying "like sheep." Logan wrote, "Not an Indian allowed in the Agency, nobody to give them medicine, no more attention paid them than dogs. It is a burning disgrace." It is no wonder that so many Paiutes turned to theft as a means of simply surviving. The Paiutes' situation did not improve under the administration of Colonel Bradfute, who was eventually removed for mismanagement and embezzlement.[30]

One cannot deny the Paiutes' importance in community dynamics during the 1870s and 1880s. The 1880 census shows St. Thomas with a population of 67. Forty-four of that total, or two-thirds of the residents, were Paiutes. If it is difficult to discern the history of St. Thomas from a non-LDS perspective after 1871, it is even harder to get the Paiute point of view, due to scarce archival material from Native American sources. What is clear is that for the Paiutes, life was hard. From 1860 to 1880, their numbers on the Muddy decreased from 500 lodges to 150 individuals. Regardless of numbers, the Paiutes represented a very valuable source of labor for whites. The Paiutes' primary interaction with whites into the twentieth century was labor at mining camps and farms. They performed menial labor at wages one-third to one-half paid to whites. One St. Thomas resident recalled that Paiutes were most important around harvest time. Until area farmers purchased a threshing machine in the 1890s, Paiute women performed the winnowing of the grain on windy days.[31] Clearly, Paiute labor continued to be important to the more heterogeneous population, as it was to the Mormon farmers in St. Thomas.

After extracting all the easy money out of the town in the 1870s, Jennings sold his claim on St. Thomas to the mercantile firm of Wooley, Lund, and Judd of St. George, which included the entire 480-acre town site. The firm attempted to turn the property into a soft-shelled-almond production zone. The attempt was a failure, and the almond trees died from lack of water. Mesquite trees reclaimed the area.[32]

Despite the greatly reduced agricultural output of St. Thomas and other Muddy settlements, farming remained one of the primary occupations. The *Deseret News* reported from Pioche in February 1873 that the new grass was six to eight inches high, wheat and barley three to four inches high, and farmers had prepared the fields to plant vegetables. Pioche residents were very interested, since the Muddy was a main source of fresh produce for the mines. Prospects must have been very good, because in March 1873 the new residents focused on clearing the irrigation ditches that had filled with sand after two seasons of disuse. The irrigation system that cost thousands of dollars to build required only a few hundred dollars to put back in working order.[33]

Daniel Bonelli benefited the most from the departure of the Saints. Shortly after the departure of the rest of the Saints, he filed for water rights in the valley, claiming one-quarter of the total flow of the Muddy, or four hundred inches. That number came from a survey completed February 1–2, 1872. The missionaries on the Muddy paid no attention to water titles, relying on church leaders to regulate its usage. Since the Saints had constructed an irrigation system, this made Bonelli's claims particularly valuable as people filtered back into the area. Bonelli raised hay and vegetables on his irrigated land, along with beef cattle, which he sold to miners in El Dorado, White Hill, and Chloride.[34]

Mining also attracted Bonelli's attention. He discovered silver in the hills around St. Thomas. Because of his discoveries and those of others who discovered placer gold nearby, miners formed the St. Thomas Mining District on January 25, 1873. He also filed claim on the salt mine near the town. According to Moapa Valley resident Sidney Whitmore, Bonelli charged $1.00 a ton if one blasted the salt oneself, $2.50 a ton for salt Bonelli had blasted beforehand. For many, the premium was worth it. One group from Mesquite who came to purchase salt watched a ledge give way and bury one of their companions, leaving only the tip of his boot hanging out.[35] Accidents aside, salt mining flourished because the mineral was in great demand by area miners who needed it for processing ore.

Once out of the ground, it was sometimes a challenge to get the salt to its destination, given the state of the roads in the area. One hauler came up with a unique solution when he ran into trouble. John Huntsman, who had broken down on his way to southern Utah, buried his salt along the route. To explain the fresh digging, he erected a crude inscription reading, "Here lies John Dillon, died of heart disease on his way to Calif." A wagon train happened to be passing by when Huntsman went to retrieve his stranded load. The train's passengers "heaped abuse" on Huntsman until they saw him throwing blocks of salt out of the hole.[36]

Even though the church abandoned the area in 1871, the proximity of so many Latter-day Saints to such large tracts of relatively unused agricultural land almost guaranteed the Muddy would not be left to miners, drifters, and outlaws. Beginning in 1880, Mormons began to come back to the Muddy to settle, this time without the church's planning and direction. The first was Elizabeth Whitmore, who bought the Patterson Ranch near Overton from Robert Patterson and his partner, E. Marshall, a one-armed Confederate veteran. In St. Thomas, Saints Harry Gentry and Edward Syphus arrived first, followed by Isaiah Cox, Jesse W. Crosby, John Monson, and Easton Kelsey. The firm of Wooley, Lund, and Judd of St. George subdivided land and sold town lots to the newcomers. Though the new settlement was not directed by the church in the same way as the first settling effort, leaders in Salt Lake were marginally involved. Church president John Taylor appointed Isaiah Cox, Jesse Crosby, and Archibald McNeil to a committee to ensure that as Mormons moved back to the Muddy on their own, they were able to obtain proper land and water titles. Arabell Hafner, in her book *100 Years on the Muddy,* asserts church leaders assigned Cox to lead a resettlement effort on the Muddy, rather than just assist with filing claims. If the church sent people, their program was much more limited than the one initiated in 1864. The 1880 census, taken right before Mormons started moving back to St. Thomas, lists twenty-three whites. Twenty years later, the census listed forty-three, a net gain of only twenty. As early as 1883, there were only two bachelors who had not sold out to the returning Mormons.[37]

With the return of the Mormons, signs of growth began appearing up and down the valley. On September 1, 1881, Lincoln County established the Virgin School District to accommodate the increased number of families with children. In 1883 there were sixteen children between the ages of six and sixteen in the area, and residents built a schoolhouse to accommodate them. It was a rough affair. One correspondent described it with pride as "12 x 16 feet in the clear, with a dirt roof, two large windows on either side, with sash and lights of the same material—light canvas—and a door and shutters of the same kind of lumber. A log about six-feet in length constitutes the school furniture—it is the half of a cottonwood log split in two."[38]

The year 1881 also saw the establishment of the Star Pony mail route. The LDS Church also established a ward in Overton, which included all the families in St. Thomas. The new Overton Ward bishop called Harry Gentry, who would be an important figure in the town's history, as his first councillor. In 1885 ward membership numbers were sufficient to establish a branch of the Young Men's Mutual Improvement Association.[39]

Part of the reason for the success of the new Mormon settlers is the church did not take such an active role in their agricultural decisions. Since they were no longer required by authorities in Salt Lake City to focus their farming attention on cotton, they could grow a more reasonable, and sustainable, range of agricultural products. Because they were also now free to associate with the Gentiles, they were also free to sell their produce to area miners, which proved a ready market.[40]

The return of Latter-day Saints to St. Thomas did not stop the town from being a haven for people avoiding law enforcement, though the character of the crimes of the fugitives was different from the decade before. In the 1880s, the federal government stepped up its prosecution of polygamists. As a youth, Willard L. Jones remembered traveling in a covered wagon through southern Utah at night to avoid officers looking for polygamists. Jones's mother was a second wife, and they were heading to the Muddy. Jones's family arrived in April 1885. Those fleeing the federal marshals considered St. Thomas out of reach of the officers because of its distance from the main settlements in Utah. It was also an appealing hiding place because most of the deputies who were seeking polygamists lacked the authority to arrest anyone outside of Utah.

The establishment of a school provided a more positive development for the town than a place to hide from the law. Some sources mention a

Mr. McGargle as a schoolteacher before 1881, but in that year Martha Cox began teaching in Overton, and all the children began going there for their lessons. In 1893 George B. Whitney moved to St. Thomas and took up the duties of schoolteacher, boarding with Daniel Bonelli and using Bonelli's parlor as a classroom. A few years later, Whitney moved the school to a boarded-up tent, where students remained until Moses Gibson's front room offered better accommodations. It was not until 1915 that St. Thomas had a dedicated school building.[41]

As the town began to regain population, its geographic location once again established St. Thomas as a supply center. John Lytle Whipple recalled that while he was working as a cattle driver for Preston Nutter, they ran out of supplies and subsisted for nearly a week on wormy peaches. His boss saddled up his horse and took a packhorse fifty miles over the mountains to St. Thomas to get supplies. When he returned with flour and coffee, Whipple and the other drivers were very happy to see him.[42] Although this is a far cry from being an essential link in the movement of people and goods that traveled around South America, it is significant that Allan Montgomery, the boss, headed not for El Dorado, Rioville, Overton, Bunkerville, Mesquite, or Kingman, but St. Thomas.

Another indication of the recovery of St. Thomas is that in the 1890s, the town was detached from the Overton Ward of the LDS Church and made into its own unit. The 1900 census shows only forty-three people in the town, but evidently authorities in Salt Lake, who would have ultimately made the decision to reestablish the ward, felt that there were enough members to support a ward. Stake leaders appointed John Bunker bishop of the reconstituted ward, joining Martin Bunker, Luke Whitney, Robert O. Gibson, and Nellie Gentry as other significant ward leaders.[43]

As St. Thomas prepared to enter the twentieth century, there were significant signs of recovery in other areas besides spiritual. The town changed from a grouping of dwellings to a full-fledged community with a nascent business district. Commercial agricultural ventures increased, and the renewed output generated discussion of a possible railroad connection to the area. This discussion was further encouraged by the mining activity in the area that used the town on the Muddy as the main source of supplies.

Although there were other stores in St. Thomas, the most important one, judging from the number of references to it in personal histories and contemporary newspaper articles, belonged to Harry Gentry. Gentry did not set out to become a store owner. In the mid-1890s, Gentry made it his custom to travel to Kingman, Arizona, to stock up on supplies he knew his family would need while he was out working as a freighter. His wife, Ellen, sold their surplus supplies to others out of the post office, for which Harry was also responsible. Gentry's store developed piecemeal from this practice.[44]

The increase in population and efforts to grow more crops for market put a strain on the water supply. The Muddy flows year-round, but it is not a particularly vigorous stream. In order to distribute the limited water equitably, the residents formed the Muddy Valley Irrigation Company in 1895. The company had fifteen thousand dollars in capital stock that was divided into fifteen thousand shares. By 1902 the company controlled 1,514 acres. Although the company water master nominally regulated water distribution, individual settlements controlled their own distribution and largely ignored the water master. St. Thomas took water from the Muddy and had six miles of canal in three ditches. These ditches irrigated 500 acres, with an average holding of 50 acres.

The major problem with the Muddy Valley Irrigation Company, aside from a limited supply of water and towns that tended to ignore its decrees, was that the only legal water right in the valley belonged to Benjamin Bonelli. Bonelli refused to join the company and consistently accused others of stealing his water. His father worked the rights he filed on in 1873 until 1879, when his tenants began to farm it. In 1894 the elder Bonelli passed control to his son. To protect his right, the younger filed suit on September 5, 1899, at Pioche, the county seat. Other valley irrigators claimed that Bonelli did not use his water to irrigate more than 10 acres and that the public good demanded they have access to the water Bonelli was otherwise letting go to waste.

The court eventually sided with Bonelli, but did not give him everything he wanted. As mentioned earlier, his father's claim totaled 400 inches, one-fourth of the flow of the river. The actual average flow of the river barely reached 240 inches. In 1893 the flow in July was 75 inches; for August it was 80, which was very different from the 1,200 Bonelli's claim was based on. The courts awarded Bonelli 60 inches in the 1890s, one-fourth of the proven maximum flow. Other irrigators could now legally water their crops.[45]

Prospects for St. Thomas and the rest of the valley at the close of the nineteenth century were much brighter than they had been in 1871. The Nevada-Utah border was firmly established, and the population slowly began to climb. Once a basic level of security was established, some residents began to, in the finest tradition of western communities, boost the area. Muddy Valley resident Jesse P. Holt claimed in his correspondence with the *Deseret News* that he was "in every way pleased with said country and [was] sanguine in the belief that home-seekers who establish themselves there can make it easy and comfortable a living as in any part of the West. The climate is semi-tropical and during ten months of the year is delightful." Another sign that the town was beginning to thrive was conversations about the prospect of the railroad passing through the valley. Although it would require concerted hard work, the idea had returned that "in a few years this valley could be transformed from its present desolate condition into a perfect garden of Eden."[46] The next two decades of growth made that idea, for many, not too far from reality.

Lost City reconstruction, 1939. The site of the Lost City is a short distance north-east of the town on the other side of the Muddy River. Courtesy of the Bureau of Reclamation, Office of Chief Engineer, Boulder Canyon Project, album 7, NARA, Denver.

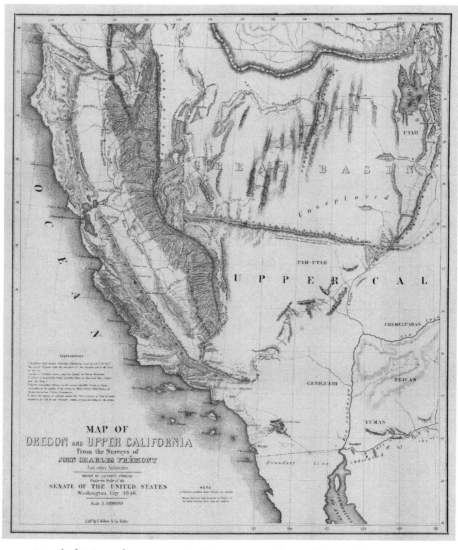

Detail of Frémont's 1848 map. St. Thomas was at the confluence shown just north of "R. Virgen" on the map. The dotted line shows Frémont's route down the Virgen and across the Muddy River. Courtesy of UNLV Special Collections.

Pioneer irrigating ditch in the Moapa Valley. Note that it seems to go through gravel, which explains why so much water was lost. Courtesy of the Boulder City Museum.

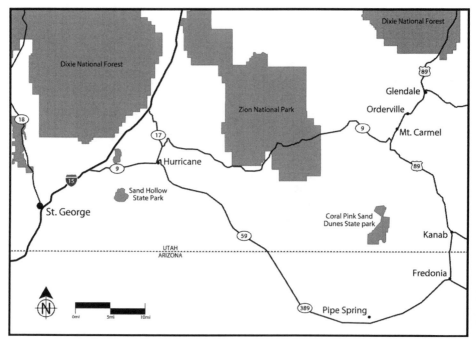

Map of southern Utah showing St. George, Glendale, and Orderville, where the Saints from the Muddy settled after they fled Nevada in 1871. Map by Brandon Hall.

TONOPAH, NEVADA, SUNDAY MORNING, AUGUST 13, 1905.

Jack Longstreet, one of the more colorful people to take up residence in St. Thomas after the Saints left. Courtesy of the *Tonopah (NV) Daily Sun,* August 13, 1905, 1:3–5.

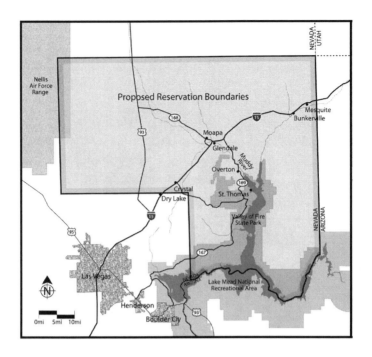

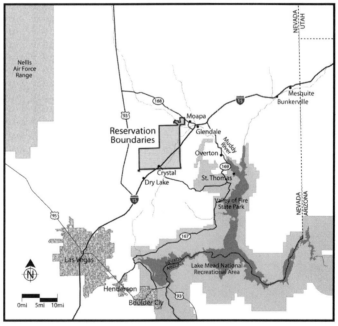

Proposed versus current reservation boundaries.
Map by Brandon Hall.

The Gentry Hotel. Courtesy of the Boulder City Museum.

St. Thomas school. Courtesy of the Boulder City Museum.

Automobile "traffic" in St. Thomas. This appears to be on the street near the Gentry Store and Gentry Hotel. Courtesy of the Boulder City Museum.

Union Pacific Railroad crew dismantling rails near St. Thomas. Courtesy of UNLV Special Collections.

St. Thomas from the air as it is slowly being covered by Lake Mead, June 1938. The large foundation near the center of the photograph is that of the school. Courtesy of the Dorothy Dorothy Collection, UNLV Special Collections.

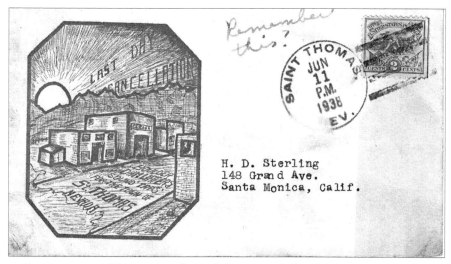

Last Day cover with a message from Whitmore to Sterling. The engraving reads "Last Day Cancellation—Boulder Dam Waters Sound 'Taps' for the Town of St. Thomas Nevada." Courtesy of the Boulder City Museum.

Albert Frehner speaking at the 1965 reunion to former St. Thomas residents and their descendants. Courtesy of the Relda Whitney Leavitt Collection, UNLV Special Collections.

5

The Mountains Brought Down and the Valleys Exalted

A. E. Cahlan, a prominent local journalist, visited the Moapa Valley in the early twentieth century. His experience shows St. Thomas entering the modern era, albeit haltingly. He described some difficulty he had in breaking a twenty-dollar note to pay a bill. He had to visit just about everyone in town to get enough change gathered together. The Moapa and Virgin Valleys were both very cash poor, and the closest bank, in terms of travel time, was in St. George. Nonbarter exchanges were accomplished using endorsed checks. Cahlan reported:

> A buyer would write a check for the amount of his purchase, say $1 or 50c. This immediately became legal tender. The merchant would give it back in change. The recipient would use it again in making his purchases. Each handler, of course, had to endorse the check. When there was no more room for an additional endorsement, the holder would take it back to the maker and have him make out a new one and start all over again. The check became sort of a negotiable promissory note not unlike the green IOU's Uncle Sam puts out today and calls them money. Checks were written for as little as 10 cents and a few ever went above $5.

During the same visit, Cahlan attended a basketball game. The only electricity available in the valley was from personal generators, and the basketball venue did not have one. The light for the night game was provided by ten to fifteen citizens standing around the court holding old-fashioned kerosene lamps on their heads.[1] Both experiences show an interesting mix of old and new.

The year 1900 marked a change in St. Thomas and the beginning of a new period on the Muddy. The town showed significant signs of recovery in population, and its economy grew at the beginning of the twentieth century. In agriculture, mining, and transportation, St. Thomas found itself emerging from the backwater and entering into a more modern world. The arrival of the railroad and the Arrowhead Trail highway brought goods and visitors in much greater numbers. Despite these advances, much of the town and its operation remained the same as they had in the century before.

The closest St. Thomas ever came to having a municipal water system was ditches running through town. Residents collected drinking water in cisterns. Electricity never arrived for lights or refrigeration, for which they used "desert coolers" consisting of wire frames covered in burlap. Water dripped onto the burlap from a reservoir overhead to keep food cool. The town never acquired a sewer system, although some residences had septic tanks. Other buildings had individual plumbing features, but none that were available to all. Several residents used the old adobe homes built by Muddy missionaries well into the twentieth century. Not all of the buildings in St. Thomas were the old adobe. Residents constructed many modern homes and businesses as well, but evidence of the hardscrabble existence shows in the improvised construction materials residents used to build their homes.

Census returns are one of the clearest indicators that the town was once again becoming viable. In 1880 the total population of St. Thomas was 67. Forty-four of those enumerated were Native American. Of the remaining 23, there were eleven surnames among them. Eight of the surnames are unique, representing a single man or woman, all listed as laborers, miners, and boarders. In 1900 the population was 43, with Native Americans enumerated elsewhere. Of the ten surnames, seven represented single men or women. There were still only three family surnames, but these three names represented many more nuclear families, as children married and stayed in town.

In 1910 the population went up to 93, but the 1920 census really shows that the town had recovered. That year the population of the town reached 170, about 75 percent of the peak population in 1868. There were only 4 single people counted, and one of those appears to be a mother-in-law. There were twenty different surnames, showing both natural growth and people moving into the town. In some ways, the town was one big family. The 1930 census illustrates this well. Of the 194 people enumerated, four surnames account for 70 of the people.[2] In the twenty years that this chapter covers, the population of the town increased 395 percent.

It is not just the total population that made a significant recovery in the twentieth century. When the Muddy missionaries left St. Thomas, the LDS population was reduced to one family. Although census returns do not list religion and the LDS Archives do not make membership rolls public, a familiarity with the stories of many of the families in the town lets the careful reader count at least part of the LDS population. In 1900, out of the total population of 43, at least 29, or 67 percent, were LDS. The percentage could have been higher, but some of the people listed are not mentioned in any available sources as LDS or not. For 1910 the number was 44 out of 93. By 1930 the total LDS population was at least 105 out of 194, which is 54 percent. The actual number was likely much higher. Regardless of the actual proportion, none of the available sources on the history of the town mentions any sort of confrontation or conflict between the Latter-day Saints and any non-LDS neighbors during this period of time.

Farming and ranching remained residents' main occupations, though the crops they grew were much different from those in the 1860s. While the town was part of the Muddy Mission, cotton, wheat, and corn received the most attention. The twentieth century brought much greater experimentation with crops. William M. Murphy, upon moving to St. Thomas in 1903, put in twenty acres of asparagus. He was the first to grow this crop on a commercial scale. Onions were another experimental commercial crop for area farmers. One reporter stated in 1908 that farmers along the Muddy grew enough onions to "perfume the breath of every girl in the United States" and were experimenting to produce an odorless variety.[3]

There were several other cash crops as well. Various farmers produced alfalfa, cantaloupes, watermelons, sugarcane, corn, sweet potatoes, peanuts, peaches, pears, grapes, pomegranates, and many other fruits and vegetables. The land was so productive that one person could handle only ten acres by himself. Another sign of modernity was that the Moapa Orchard and Fruit Company seriously contemplated the construction of a hydroelectric plant on the Muddy. Nothing ever came of the plans to build the dam, but it certainly would have been welcome not only for the electricity, but also for flood control. Floods in 1910 and 1914 wiped out crops and fences, as well as damaged a railroad right-of-way.[4]

Many in St. Thomas engaged in animal husbandry. Frank Bonelli, George Pearson, and Brig Whitmore grazed 250 head of cattle along the Muddy River. Sam Gentry and his partner from Utah, Warren Cox, ran 2,000 head on the Gold Butte Range during these years. Horses were especially important, since they performed farmwork and transportation duties. Not all the horses in the area were domesticated. Matilda Frehner had fond memories of working with the wild horses in the area. She remembered that the horses were almost economically valueless, because they were so small and skinny. Matilda remembered that when she was twelve, she convinced one of the cowboys who had rounded up some of the horses to give her one. It ended up being her favorite horse for a long time.[5]

The church's injunction against mining did not survive into the twentieth century. Many devout members of the church engaged in mining with just as much zeal as their Gentile counterparts. Several of the residents of the town operated successful mining operations. In 1905 the *Salt Lake Mining Review* expressed excitement about the prospects of the new St. Thomas Mining District. Prospectors struck gold at the base of Granite Mountain, across the Virgin River from St. Thomas, and the *Review* was certain that a rush was imminent. Interestingly, residents of St. Thomas knew about the deposits at Gold Butte and Granite Mountain, but not being miners, they did not realize the true value of the deposits that were in their backyard.[6]

It did not take long for locals to begin to take note of the mining possibilities the area held. In an article entitled "St. Thomas to the Front," the *Salt Lake Mining Review* speculated that the town was part of an immense mineral zone extending from Searchlight to Goldfield, and a boom in the area was very likely.[7] Residents wanted to capitalize early on the possibilities. One of the great mineral finds in the area was discovered by an associate of Harry Gentry.

Gentry's associate was prospecting in limestone near the Gold Butte and Granite Mountain camps. After working all day and finding nothing of apparent value, he sat on a boulder to rest, discouraged. While sitting there, he unconsciously began feeling the rock with his fingers. Feeling a formation crumble, he looked at the rock and noticed a small copper seam. He put up a marker and did the work required by Nevada law to make a claim. A few days later, he began to work the claim. He followed the seam in from the face for about a foot when he broke into a large body of fine copper. After working the site for a week, he had enough ore to fill two railcars. The ore turned out to contain 64.8 percent copper. This strike was not Gentry's last foray into mining, as a few years later Harry and Ellen Gentry, Levi and Clara Syphus, and Nellie Perkins incorporated the Bronzel Mining Company in St. Thomas, capitalized with one million one-dollar shares.[8]

Ellen Gentry had a particularly strange experience with mining. According to legend, one morning she awoke with a very odd feeling about a dream she had about a nearby borax deposit. Her dream was so vivid that she and her daughter Laura grubstaked two prospectors to search for the "dream mine." The prospectors followed Ellen's details and found a gulch with a large exposed face of borax. Francis "Borax" Smith, the man behind the twenty-mule teams in Death Valley, learned of the discovery and purchased the mine. This mine did not require twenty mules to haul the borax, being much closer to the rail line than the Death Valley deposits.[9]

When St. Thomas collapsed in 1871, Overton became the mercantile center for the valley. With the beginning of the new century, however, St. Thomas began to show significant signs of recovery in that industry as well. The year 1907 saw the construction of a new store in St. Thomas and the increased availability of goods. This and Harry Gentry's store caused one observer to remarked that it "looks as if this country must be coming to the front."[10]

By 1918 there were a handful of other businesses in town. Rhiner Hannig operated a grocery store and soda fountain. Preston Nutter also ran a grocery store. Ellen Gentry ran a hotel that was located next to the Gentry store. The town had a post office, and William Sellers operated a café, which also carried groceries geared toward tourists. Henry Howell operated a garage, and Rox Whitmore owned a meat market from which he supplied the valley with fresh beef and pork. Whitmore even made deliveries as far as Las Vegas and Arden, which is now part of Las Vegas, but farther south on the way to Pahrump.[11] The 1910 and 1920 censuses also listed a professional photographer, Frederick G. Rance, with a studio in town.

Although St. Thomas was slowly recovering economically, it still faced significant challenges. The Saints left the town in 1871, in part due to their inability to pay taxes in specie. Decades later, the area remained cash poor, barter remaining the preferred method of carrying out financial transactions for many people, as evidenced by the experience of A. E. Cahlan, mentioned at the beginning of the chapter. Economic difficulties or no, it was the businesses run by the Gentrys, however, that were the most important in town. Harry was the postmaster, so people would congregate at the store in the afternoons and socialize while they were waiting for the mail buggy from Moapa. The fourteen-room Gentry Hotel was a popular gathering place as well, hosting important guests like US senator Key Pittman and Nevada governors Tasker Oddie and James Scrugham on different occasions.[12] Such august visitors were not the norm, though. Most customers were residents of the town or the immediate surrounding area.

Beyond being a successful businessman, Harry Gentry was also a community pillar. He moved to St. Thomas from Panaca in 1883 with Ellen and was almost immediately made the local postmaster, a position he held until he died. When he died, he was the oldest postmaster in the state. He also held many positions of importance in the St. Thomas Ward of the LDS Church. Martin A. Bunker, one of his friends, said he never knew a more charitable man in his life. Harry once caught a man stealing from his store. The local justice court tried and convicted the man, but rather than see him go to jail, Harry loaned the man forty dollars to pay the fine. Gentry also had a soft spot for children. The young Joe F. Perkins asked Harry for the job of mail carrier to Bonelli's Ferry. Perkins was not old enough to work legally for the government, but he must have been extremely persistent in his pleading. Gentry finally said, "Alright, Joe, how old are you?" "Ten," said Joe. "Ah, no," Gentry said, "you're sixteen," and proceeded to swear Joe in.[13]

The Church of Jesus Christ of Latter-day Saints remained the most important institution in town. Available sources are silent on what happened to the church building with the hand-split shingles after the abandonment of the town, though it is likely that Isaac Jennings dismantled and sold it. Regardless of what happened, in the early 1900s the faithful met in a boarded-up tent. Doris Reber lived across the street from the rudimentary chapel. She told John Bunker, who became bishop of the ward in September 1908, that she did not want to go to church. She said she might as well stay home because she could hear him just as well across the street, as he talked so loudly.[14] With streets ninety-nine feet wide, his voice must have been penetrating indeed.

Members of the church's women's auxiliary, the Relief Society, decided they would like a nicer place to meet. They decided they would fund the construction of a Relief Society hall. In order to raise the money for the hall, they held a series of ice cream socials. On the day of a social, they made ice cream from eggs, cream, and their carefully hoarded sugar. In the evening, they brought their husbands and children and used their "pin money" to purchase their own ice cream. They counted themselves very blessed when freighters from the Grand Gulch Mine were in town and in the mood to spend money. After all the fund-raisers were over and the hall completed, it served triple duty. It held school and church meetings as well as Relief Society meetings.[15]

Although St. Thomas lay on the periphery of lands controlled by the Saints, general authorities of the church did not ignore the congregation. Apostles and other leaders came to conduct church business when the rail line opened. They also made periodic visits when there were not any significant events occurring. Everett Syphus's history recorded a chance encounter with George Albert Smith, who at the time was an apostle but later became the president of the church. Syphus was out working in the field one hot day when he saw two men walking toward him, whom he discovered to be Smith and his son. They were very hot and thirsty, having been stuck in the sand and working in vain to free their wagon, which had become mired in the Virgin. Syphus felt honored to take his team and help an apostle out of a tight spot.[16] Other visits by church leaders transpired with less drama.

The Paiutes remained a constant presence in and around St. Thomas, though armed confrontations did not. Inez Gibson Waymire, daughter of Bishop Robert O. Gibson, claimed that not many Paiutes actually lived on the reservation, but camped in tepees by the "Big Ditch." The Paiute men and women continued as a valuable source of labor. The men worked as farm laborers or as maintenance workers on the irrigation works. White women hired the Paiute women to wash laundry, scrubbing the clothes on washboards outside. The group had not become sedentary, though. In the fall, the entire encampment would move to the mountains and gather pine nuts. They sold their surplus to the townspeople or wholesale to the Gentry store. At Christmastime, residents were usually visited by a Paiute woman who would knock on the door and hold out a sack saying "Christmas gift," expecting flour, bacon, or whatever happened to be on hand. Although they may have been on the fringes of the white community, they were included in every large community celebration. Paiutes came from miles around, especially when there was a barbecue, taking away any leftover meat or bones.

One Paiute couple received particular attention in many residents' diaries, Maud and Curley. Curley, the woman, was mean and cantankerous. Her husband, Maud, was blind, and she would lead him around by tying a rope around his neck. This probably was not too bad, except that she would ride their horse while he ran alongside. Stowell Whitney came upon them one day to discover Curley burying Maud alive. Poor Maud was squirming at the bottom of the hole under the weight of the dirt. Whitney objected, saying, "You can't bury him alive," while pulling Maud out of the hole. Curley replied, "Better be dead than starve to death." Whitney spent a few moments filling the hole back in, gave the unhappy couple all the food he had, and sent them on their way.[17]

As more whites moved into the area, the traditional ways of the Paiutes became less viable as a means of support. Consequently, the Paiutes became even more dependent on wage labor, and it is not a good idea to antagonize one's employers. George Perkins, a local observer of the Paiutes, told a story of how the presence of whites influenced them. Early Paiutes, after burying their dead, would take all the deceased's possessions and burn them. If the departed had a horse, then relatives and friends killed it so the departed would have a mount in the afterlife. One young Paiute watched over an older one, who in return made the young man heir to his estate, which comprised a few acres of land and two good horses. When the man died, tribal elders expected the young man to sacrifice the horses. Instead, he burned an old Model T that had given him considerable trouble. He said, "When all the Indians come riding up on horses in the next world, old John will drive up in that Model T and be just as well off as any of them!"[18]

For many towns in the West, a primary place to gather and socialize was some kind of bar, which St. Thomas did not have at this point. Adult entertainment in St. Thomas during this period was predictably scarce. Adults would gather at the Gentry store, waiting for the mail, and gossip. It was there that "all the town problems were solved." Not all entertainment was just talking to neighbors. Preston Nutter had a crystal radio set in the back of his grocery store. The kids would line up for a chance to listen to it for a few minutes, relishing the time they spent with the headphones on their heads. Mr. Hannig showed the first motion pictures in town in the Relief Society hall. The machine that showed the silent movies was hand cranked and suffered frequent breakdowns. Despite this, those who attended were fine with spending their twenty-five cents on admission. Residents celebrated holidays with dances, horse races, relay races, and baseball and basketball games. Horse races in particular were subject to intense betting. Baseball games were more relaxed. The young women played the married women, and the young men would play the married men. The youth particularly enjoyed watermelon bursts. Euzell Prince Preston recalled that at such activities, all the boys would catch a girl and wash her hair in watermelon rinds.[19]

Children enjoyed cart rides, playing in the ditches, sledding down sandy hills on boards, playing "run sheep run," and other common youthful pursuits. The lives of the children of St. Thomas, however, were not all carefree. Being a farming community, there were always chores that needed attention. At one point, the town was experiencing an infestation of rodents, and the youth played an important role in the eradication effort. Katherine Perkins, a schoolteacher, spearheaded efforts to eliminate gophers, rats, and mice. She divided the boys from first through sixth grades into two teams. The first side to get three hundred tails treated themselves to a candy pull hosted by the losers. Mrs. Perkins verified the number of tails. One first grader thought that they were interested only in the tails, so he cut them off and released the mice to grow more tails for future harvesting.[20]

Life in St. Thomas was not always idyllic, but it was a close community nonetheless. Neighbors planted and harvested each other's fields and treated wagons and threshers as community property. The only town government was a school board. The town required no police or jail. All civic leadership was performed by church leaders.[21] Residents united themselves in the promotion of their town, excited by the advances made in transportation to and from St. Thomas.

Merle Frehner, a prominent Las Vegan who died in 1994, is most widely remembered as a good businessman and founder of the Boulder Dam Area Council, now the Las Vegas Area Council, of the Boy Scouts of America. Less remembered is that he was an expert in hauling freight in wagons with six-horse teams. In interviews and remembrances, Frehner painted a vivid picture of just how difficult it was to move goods from one place to another. Trains consumed water and wood or coal only when moving. The same holds true for gasoline and automobiles. Horses, however, required water and forage whether they were working or not, and they could not be "parked" for a week while work was done. One of the first issues of the *Las Vegas Age* reveled in the arrival of automobiles in the Bullfrog Mining District in 1905, but early vehicles were not suited to haul heavy loads. Long distances from railheads over poor roads with no gas stations kept freight wagons and teams rumbling across southern Nevada well into the twentieth century.

Frehner's 1918 account of one freighting trip illustrates just how difficult the process could be. Merle and his brother Harry contracted to haul heavy machinery fifty miles to the Grand Gulch mine from St. Thomas. The brothers removed the bed from their biggest wagon and replaced it with heavy timbers upon which they chained the equipment. Before leaving they had to plan carefully to provide for the team of twelve horses required for the one-hundred-mile round-trip through the desert. No doubt the brothers were glad that they were not hauling the freight into St. Thomas. Crossing the Virgin River could be very dangerous, and many loads were lost attempting to cross in high water. To minimize that danger, the county built a steel bridge across the Virgin River in 1915, but the freighters then had to maneuver their six- to twelve-ton loads down a steep slope to get to the bridge. If the water was low, many preferred to take the river route and avoid the very real possibility of their wagons going out of control and crashing.[22] Given the difficult experience of freighters, it is no wonder so many wanted modern transportation in the area.

The arrival of the railroad marked St. Thomas's strategic location within southern Nevada. Securing a rail line into the town was a coup of the highest order for the town. Many localities better situated than St. Thomas had to resort to bribery to have a line located in their towns. Because railroads were more interested in profits than in any town's welfare, the decision demonstrates the faith they had in St. Thomas. Although Brigham Young had envisioned St. Thomas as a key link in the transportation of people and goods from the Colorado River north to Utah, he probably never envisioned the construction of a rail line there. President Young's nephew Joseph W. Young certainly never foresaw rail access for the town. He wrote of the area in 1868, "The timber and the mineral [in the soil] may be partially overcome, but the bad roads never, at least not till the mountains are brought down and the valleys exalted, and the sand hills and sand-beds covered with brush."[23]

Assistant church historian Andrew Jensen mentioned the possibility of a railroad into the Moapa Valley as early as 1892, but not until 1908 did it even begin to look like St. Thomas had a chance. By 1905 Moapa, twenty-five miles from St. Thomas on the north end of the valley, connected to the Salt Lake line. Residents to the south engaged in the same self-promotion as almost every community in the West. Oil started the discussion in earnest. In February 1908, Standard Oil began exploration near Overton. If crews struck oil, promoters envisioned the inevitable rail line from Moapa extending all the way down the valley to St. Thomas. According to the *Las Vegas Age*, farmers believed this would enable the entire valley to easily provide produce for oil workers.[24]

Other boosters looked to expand industries that already existed in the valley. One company believed that of the four hundred thousand tons of salt consumed yearly along the Pacific Coast, the salt mines near St. Thomas could produce a significant part of it, up to twenty-five thousand pounds a day. Farmers and those engaged in home manufacture wanted the greater access to markets. Miners of gypsum, pottery clay, copper, silver, and gold would all benefit from the arrival of the iron horse. Still others who were lobbying for a state experimental farm to be built on the Muddy felt their enterprise could only be strengthened by a rail line. The groups differed on if they should wait for a major rail line to build there or seek the construction of a cheaper narrow-gauge line to expedite the process.[25]

In order to bring their plans to fruition, different groups lobbied railroad executives and capitalists in different ways. The *Las Vegas Age* reported in February 1908 that a group contemplating increased salt production sent a representative to New York in an attempt to get funding to build the rail line. A. L. F. MacDermott, secretary of both the Moapa Valley Farmer's Association and the Muddy Valley Irrigation Company, commissioned a survey in 1909 for a branch railroad from Moapa to St. Thomas so that when the anticipated funds were secured, there would be little need for delay in starting construction.[26]

It was not until 1911, however, that the efforts of the railroad boosters began to pay off, beginning with a meeting between E. J. Robertson, manager of Moapa Valley's Irrigation and Development Company, and Senator William A. Clark of Montana. Clark was also president of the San Pedro, Los Angeles & Salt Lake Railroad, a subsidiary of the Union Pacific Railroad, which was the line that ran through Moapa.[27] He was an important figure in the history of southern Nevada and a controversial one in the history of the United States. A consummate businessman, Clark experienced a series of early successes in business, the largest being the Anaconda Copper Company in Butte, Montana. He achieved national prominence in 1899 when he bribed the Montana state legislature to appoint him senator. Upon arriving in Washington, Clark realized that the Senate would never seat him, so he resigned, creating a vacancy. The governor of Montana, who disliked Clark, was out of the state at the time, so the lieutenant governor, who was more kindly disposed to Clark, hastened eight hundred miles back to Helena to appoint Clark senator again. The governor rescinded the appointment and chose another man. The Senate refused to seat either man. This episode helped clear the way for the passage of the Seventeenth Amendment to the Constitution in 1913, which provided for the direct election of senators. Clark eventually won a seat in the Senate in 1901, this time legitimately.

Clark built the San Pedro, Los Angeles & Salt Lake line because it decreased the distance between his mines in Montana and a working seaport by 663 miles. Clark and E. H. Harriman of the Union Pacific and Oregon Short Line survived an uneasy partnership to complete the line in 1905. Clark's line purchased the land for the town site of Las Vegas from Helen Stewart, who owned the Las Vegas Ranch. The ranch started as the Mormon Fort on Las Vegas Creek. Clark and his brother tried to diversify the economy of the new town beyond railroad repair yards. Indeed, his brother J. Ross Clark actively promoted Las Vegas until his death in 1927. It was in honor of William Clark's efforts that the new county created by the division of Lincoln County in 1909 received the name Clark County.

The spur down the Muddy was supposed to go only as far south as Logandale, previously known as St. Joseph. In his meeting with Clark, Robertson waxed rhapsodic about the potential of St. Thomas. He discussed the salt and kaolin deposits, as well as the agricultural output, which improved market access would only increase. The reality was probably more prosaic, but Robertson reported, "When the real facts were brought before Senator Clark he lost no time in authorizing the construction of the line on from Logan." Farmers immediately began putting in more crops than they had originally planned for that year, though it would be another year before the rails actually reached the town. Residents had known the good news barely two weeks when some began to speculate that the line would not really terminate at St. Thomas, but would follow the Virgin River up to St. George.[28]

Three months before the projected completion of the line to St. Thomas, the Las Vegas Chamber of Commerce already had a plan to celebrate the event. The plan was to run a special train from Las Vegas to St. Thomas, stopping at all the scenic areas along the way. The goal was to "give many people of Vegas who have never seen the wonderful Moapa valley a chance to visit it on a pleasant occasion at small cost, and partake of the open handed hospitality of the valley people." It was also seen as an opportunity to showcase the agricultural output of the area. Construction delays thwarted the initial plans of the organizers, but the papers continued to track the builders' progress and speculated on the completion date. As it turned out, the rails reached the town at the end of March 1912, though it was a month and a half before the line officially opened.[29]

Boosters and farmers were not the only ones excited by the imminent prospect of the rail line into St. Thomas. Salt miners thought the easy access to better transportation would make them major players in their market. St. Thomas resident and principal owner of the Tramp mine Brig Whitmore, owners of the Key West mine, and the Los Angeles-based Copper City mine managers were waiting only for the completion of the line to begin shipping ore. All three mines already had large quantities of ore stockpiled and ready to go.[30]

In late May 1912, when it became apparent when the line would open, plans began again for a celebration to mark the event. The Majestic Theatre in Las Vegas held a "Queen of the Rail" contest to see who the most popular woman in the county was. The winner would win an expense-paid trip to St. Thomas as an honored guest and the privilege of driving the final spike. The Grand Gulch Copper Company provided the copper spike for the occasion. The queen would use a "handsome" hammer, provided by the Salt Lake Hardware Company, and receive the hammer and spike as souvenirs at the close of the festivities. The prospect of gaining recognition as the most popular woman proved sufficient to "make the ladies' hearts to flutter." The honor fell to local resident Mildred Anderson, apparently a Las Vegan.[31]

Ms. Anderson drove that last spike on June 1, 1912. The Las Vegas Chamber of Commerce organized an excursion train to St. Thomas. After leaving Las Vegas, it proceeded to Logan (later Logandale) to allow for the brief inspection of the state experiment farm. From there it went to Overton, which by now was the most populous town on the Muddy, and then on to St. Thomas for the festivities. At St. Thomas, in addition to the spike-driving ceremony, there was a southern barbecue to "fill the inner man to overflowing with all manner of good things," followed by a ball game, steer-roping competition, and other sports. At five in the evening, the train would depart for Overton and a dance held there. Return to Las Vegas was to commence at 11:00 p.m. for the hour and a half trip back. Passengers could even expect to have a pleasant time while on the train. During the train ride and at various stops, the Las Vegas Brass Band, which would make the journey as well, would entertain passengers. Mayor Buol of Las Vegas called on all residents to take the day off and spend it on the Muddy to "congratulat[e] . . . our northern neighbors on the new era of prosperity which must come to them following the advent of railway transportation for their products." His call fell on willing ears, as about two hundred, or one-quarter of the population of Las Vegas, expected to make the trip.[32]

The arrival of the railroad was a harbinger that the area had "arrived" in many ways. The festivities were attended by the president of the Quorum of the Twelve Apostles of the LDS Church, Francis M. Lyman, and apostle George F. Richards, as well as O. P. Miller of the Presiding Bishopric of the church. D. T. Collet, secretary of the Utah Manufacturers Association, accompanied the church leaders. While there, the church leaders created a new stake, named the Moapa Stake, from the wards in St. Thomas, Overton, Panaca, Mesquite, Bunkerville, and Alamo. The visiting authorities also called Robert O. Gibson as bishop of the St. Thomas Ward, where he remained until the disbanding of the ward.[33]

The arrival of the railroad brought some changes to St. Thomas, the newly christened "Terminal Town." The refrigerated cars brought ice, which allowed residents to replace their wood, wire, and burlap desert coolers with iceboxes. However, the rails brought more than ice. Improved access allowed the casual tourist easy access to the south end of the Muddy. The railroad published tourist tracts to encourage this trend. Not all of the people who came down the rails were entirely welcome, though. Ed Syphus had a patch of melons by the railroad grade, and the railroad workers frequently stole them. One night while the train was stopped, he went up to the patch and fired his gun in the air, causing the workers to scatter quickly.[34]

As the boosters had hoped, the railroad proved to be a benefit to the area's major industries. T. O. Tolan, Benjamin Bonelli, Levi Syphus, Harry Gentry, and H. E. George organized the Virgin River Salt Company in 1908, but they recognized that the venture was not viable until the railroad arrived. After the completion of the line, the papers contained periodic reports of large shipments of salt from the St. Thomas salt mine. By 1926 the company was shipping a carload of salt a day. The agricultural sector also greatly benefited from the railroad. Although many crops grew well on the Muddy, cantaloupes and watermelons became a major cash crop.[35]

Area miners warmly welcomed the railroad as well. The Grand Gulch mine freighted its ore to St. Thomas, which saved their heavy wagons a much longer trip up the Muddy. The mine was profitable, as prices were high and the ore ran as high as 56 percent copper. The new line cut the distance to the railhead by a third, which was very welcome for its effect on the bottom line.[36]

Completion of the railroad highlighted talk about rail-related improvements in St. Thomas. In 1913 the Nevada State Railway Commission approved the issue of $1,119,000 in bonds to pay for improved locomotives and rolling stock, earmarking about a third of the funds for the line to St. Thomas. Also in 1913, the Southwestern Pacific Railroad incorporated in Sacramento, California. The $105 million road would be twenty-two hundred miles long and run between Denver and San Diego and through St. Thomas. Like so many other railroad lines in the West, this one never made it past the planning stages. In 1915 San Pedro, Los Angeles & Salt Lake Railroad engineers surveyed a line between St. Thomas and the area gypsum mines but never constructed it. Another paper railroad contemplated a line through Mohave County, Arizona, from Kingman to St. Thomas in 1917.[37]

Having successfully secured railroad access, St. Thomas residents began to turn their attention to other ways to link themselves to the outside world. A mere ten months after the driving of the last spike, St. Thomas residents told reporters, "[We] have good lands, [we] want good roads." They earnestly sought to have a modern highway pass through their town. Automobiles did not have nearly the freight capacity of railroads, but had much greater flexibility. One of the first things the residents did was to send Joseph Ira Earl and William E. Abbott from the Muddy to Salt Lake City to attend a meeting of the Salt Lake Auto Club and sing the praises of an auto route running through St. Thomas to Los Angeles. They probably did not have to talk too hard to convince the people in Salt Lake that the route through southern Utah was the best one, since the other possible route went through Ely, Goldfield, and Bishop and added considerable distance to the trek. The Los Angeles-to-Denver distance via St. Thomas shortened the trip by four hundred miles and was serviceable year-round.[38]

Despite the new railroad, obtaining good roads remained important to St. Thomas residents, given the poor condition of existing wagon tracks. The Grand Gulch Mining Company purchased the first truck in St. Thomas and shipped it to the lower Muddy by rail. The man the company sent to drive the truck dressed in a glowing black duster, goggles, fancy leggings, and other finery. The entire town turned out to see the truck unloaded. When the truck backed off the railcar, its hard rubber tires sunk into the sand, rendering the vehicle stationary. The company needed a team of horses to haul it down the street. All the kids in town climbed into the back of it and took a ride. Beyond tires unsuited for the territory, the motor ran hot, the brakes smoked coming down the canyon, and a six-mile stretch of sharp lime rocks on the route to the mine destroyed the tires. The truck managed only three trips to the mine before it was shipped out of the area.[39] Although the machine was clearly unsuited for service in the desert, good roads would likely have allowed the mining company to continue to use it.

Within four months of Earl and Abbott's trip to Salt Lake, Clark County commissioners used St. Thomas as their base of operations to scout the best route for the new road. The topic frequently made the papers for the rest of the year, and public opinion throughout the entire county viewed the construction of the road favorably. Stories about the contemplated highway frequently graced the front pages of area newspapers. Because of the cost, however, in a county commissioners' meeting in March 1914, the commissioners decided that the time was not right to begin building it. Commissioner Bunker from St. Thomas raised the sole voice to try to keep the plan for the road alive.[40]

The commissioners were reticent not because they considered the road a bad idea, but because of the route dictated by geography. Several miles of the road would pass through the northwest corner of Arizona, which would be of absolutely no benefit to that state. Consequently, Mohave County officials refused to spend any money on it. Clark County and Mohave County officials reached a compromise. Mohave County would provide the funds to complete the road through the corner of its state, while Clark County built south from St. Thomas to Bonelli's Ferry on the Colorado to connect with the Arizona system of roads. This route would utilize the $13,500 bridge over the Virgin near St. Thomas then currently under construction. By the middle of 1915, the Arrowhead Trail highway was a reality.[41]

As with the opening of the railroad, St. Thomas hosted a party to celebrate the completion of the Arrowhead Trail. The Southern Nevada Automobile Club joined with the Las Vegas Chamber of Commerce to promote the excursion to the Muddy, held on May 30, 1915. The group planned to leave Las Vegas at six in the morning and arrive in St. Thomas three to four hours later, depending on the road. St. Thomas residents provided a barbecue to fete the visitors. Those without a car received an invitation to come, and for a small fee they could ride along.[42]

The report of the trip was front-page news in Las Vegas. Although the road was not in the best condition, Las Vegans made the fifty-seven-mile trip in just over four hours without mishap. A crowd that had gathered in a bowery in Harry Gentry's yard met the excursionists, who received ice water and lemonade. Chair of the Clark County Commission C. C. Ronnow presided at their ceremony and made a plea to all the people there that they would cooperate with the county in keeping the roads repaired and in good condition. Nevada Democratic Party leader Levi Syphus spoke as well. At the close of the meeting, the audience sang "The Star-Spangled Banner" and "America."[43]

The railroad was extremely important to the economy of the area, but because the line to St. Thomas was a spur line, there was no traffic "just passing through." The completion of the Arrowhead Trail changed that. St. Thomas began to gain recognition outside the region as it became apparent that it sat on the best route from the interior of the country to the Pacific Coast.

Earl Anthony and his car, Cactus Kate, gained St. Thomas much of that recognition. Earl was a member of the Automobile Club of Southern California, one of the earliest such clubs in the country. His black, gold, white, and red Packard 5-48 stunt car made several trips north from Los Angeles, and his exploits were reported in the *Los Angeles Times.* His travel accounts and pictures helped greatly to popularize the Arrowhead Trail. A year after the road opened, Anthony waxed rhapsodic about the road in Clark County. He penned, "Of all the desert roads of the great Southwest none holds such a wonderful sight present in such a dramatic manner as the Arrowhead trail between Las Vegas and St. Thomas at which latter place the Cactus Kate party arrived tonight." He found more than the road leading up to the town agreeable. St. Thomas impressed him as well. He penned, "St. Thomas at the end of today's run is a beautiful little town that nestles under the huge cottonwoods in the bottom lands of the Big Muddy River." Anthony was also very impressed with the scenery between St. Thomas and St. George and speculated that the eroded sandstone would prove to be a powerful tourist draw. He had high praise for the residents he met along the way, saying that "nowhere in the United States could be found a more loyal set of skilled road workers" than he found along the Arrowhead Trail.[44]

Other travelers expressed pleasure with the area as well. One enjoyed his foray into Mormon country because "wherever one goes in the United States, one will not find a kindlier or more hospitable people." C. H. Biglow mirrored these sentiments in an article in *Arrowhead Magazine.* Biglow noted, "When you get among the Mormons you are in good hands."[45]

Not every Arrowhead Trail traveler was as impressed with St. Thomas. The reason was the same one that travelers had complained about for the previous two centuries: the weather. One person from central Utah passing through the area had the following to say about the environment:

> January in this country is equivalent to a mild March in Utah, and the parallel holds good until July, when Hades is a refrigerator by comparison. During July and August the box-washes are veritable ovens, and those who are compelled to traverse them under a southern Nevada sun will never forget their experience. . . . While you are in Utah are blowing your fingers to keep them warm and walking around in a ten pound overcoat, we are fighting green flies, killing tarantulas, keeping a wary lookout for deadly sidewinders, and going about in our shirt sleeves. . . . There are ten million flies and twenty million mosquitoes to each of the three hundred residents of the Muddy Valley, and with even that proportion of flies are kept busy keeping the inhabitants awake during daylight, and the mosquitoes compel them to take some exercise during the night.[46]

The road did make things better for heat-sensitive travelers, if only because it allowed them to travel through the area much more quickly than a horse-drawn wagon was capable.

Hospitality was important to make travelers feel welcome, but even more important was road maintenance, which could be a challenge without full-time work crews on unpaved roads. The lack of state funds supporting the roads made it even more difficult. This lack led many to the conviction that there was a funding bias for roads around Carson City. Although this may or may not have been true, the papers show that the state road commission did move at a glacial pace in approving projects in the South. Other times the weather did not cooperate, as in 1916, when flooding on the Virgin River washed out sixty feet of the approach to the bridge near the town. Fortunately, the steel span escaped damage.[47]

The county secured sufficient funds in 1917 to build a road from St. Thomas to Moapa and improve the road to Mesquite. Road workers used St. Thomas as their base of operations for the work. In 1918 residents took maintenance on the road upon themselves to keep it in good shape for tourists and other travelers. Residents declared March 8–9, 1919, "road days," and turned out with rakes and shovels to rake off the loose rock and fill the chuckholes.[48]

The people of the town recognized the advantages the road brought and were not about to lose them through their inattention. When the town found itself in danger, it was not poor road maintenance that was the cause, but decisions made by bureaucrats on the other side of the country. The first indicator that something was coming was in the summer of 1919, when Osborn Gentry traveled thirty miles on horseback to deliver a telegram to Harry Armitage, a Colorado River boatman, from the US Bureau of Reclamation.[49] The news he brought would eventually make two decades of business, highways, and railroads seem to be of little consequence.

6

Not with a Bang, but a Whimper

In St. Thomas, the twenties started out in a fairly encouraging fashion. In March 1921, the county completed a bridge over the Virgin River at Mesquite. The opening celebration almost depopulated Mesquite, Bunkerville, St. Thomas, Overton, and Logandale, for the day, and saw many attend from Las Vegas as well. Nearly two thousand attended the bridge opening, which was presided over by the bishop of the Mesquite Ward. The stake president and another bishop spoke at the ceremony, and the stake patriarch dedicated the bridge. The bridge made traveling the Arrowhead Trail through the area much more pleasant. However, 1921 proved to be the last year that transportation seemed promising on the Arrowhead Trail for St. Thomas residents. In August 1921, flooding rendered the bridge across the Virgin River at St. Thomas useless. The steel span escaped damage, but the approach on the east side succumbed to the torrent.[1] This mix of elation and disappointment characterized the whole decade of the 1920s for the town.

Boosters reveled in the abundant signs of progress in the Moapa Valley. Not all progress boded well for St. Thomas, however, especially the decision of Congress to build the Hoover Dam. Because of its proximity to the proposed dam sites, St. Thomas served as a base of operations for survey crews. Even though those continuing surveys made it apparent to residents that the town's days were numbered, they continued to boost the town. Boosters' efforts were rewarded richly with the discovery of the Lost City-Anasazi ruins right outside the town—and then a pageant in its celebration.

The discovery could not prevent the relocation of the highway far to the north of the town and certainly did not slow the survey of lands for government purchase and the resolving of mining claims. Most mining claims were settled relatively smoothly, but the property appraisal board quickly split into two factions and created the basis for years of legal wrangling and acrimonious discussion. By the end of the appraisal process, the town was largely abandoned.

Although the people of St. Thomas did not realize that this was the case, the telegram to Harry Armitage signaled the town's death knell. The Bureau of Reclamation contracted Armitage to carry survey crews on the Colorado in preparation of the construction of a dam. The survey was headed by H. L. Baldwin and assisted by St. Thomas residents Hugh Lord, Ernest Ward, and Sam Gentry, who were chosen in part because their "interests [were] not particularly involved." Although the decision to place the dam in Black Canyon rather than Boulder Canyon had yet to be made, it was clear that whatever the dam site, both could bring the water to the 1,250-foot contour line and inundate both St. Thomas and the small nearby community of Kaolin.

Baldwin's initial report was not very flattering toward St. Thomas and the surrounding area. He noted that because the amount of annual rainfall was very small, only the hardiest plants were capable of surviving unaided. He said that "even cactus in its various forms is quite scarce. . . . [S]agebrush, that almost universal habitant of the desert hardly occurs at all." The cattle appeared to be undernourished, being forced to subsist on the meager forage or on grain that had to be shipped in by rail.

Baldwin was derisive of area farming. He reported that residents grew wheat, alfalfa, grapes for raisins, cantaloupe, and some garden vegetables, but "none . . . seem profitable, and the community . . . is far from being a thrifty, enterprising, or successful one." There was land that he felt could have been productively farmed but was neglected. He was even critical of the irrigation system, saying that bad management had reduced its effectiveness to almost nothing. His estimate of the total value for all improvements, houses, fences, ditches, and irrigable lands up the Muddy and the Virgin from the confluence of the two streams was less than $450,000. This estimate did not include the value of railway property. Irrigated land, he claimed, deserved no more than $125 an acre. Subsequent government representatives agreed with Baldwin's low estimation of the area.[2]

Recognizing the preliminary nature of his survey, Baldwin included with his report some advice for future survey crews. He listed the nearest dependable store to obtain supplies as Harry Gentry's store and described Harry as unusually obliging and well informed about the country. He also reported that a route through St. Thomas was the best way to reach the proposed reservoir site.[3] As the survey crews that followed heeded his advice, the town benefited economically from the increased traffic.

Merle Frehner remembered that there were several survey crews that came and made St. Thomas their base of operations, each staying for several months. They used the town for more than lodging and a supply depot. It was also the place where surveyors hired local help. In November 1921, the *Las Vegas Age* reported that the US Reclamation Service was planning to run three drilling outfits to work at Boulder Canyon. The bureau brought in drill runners from the outside, but required about twenty "good husky" men for laborers, with the hiring done in St. Thomas. There is no record of how many responded; the pay the bureau was offering was good for the time, $3.75 a day, minus $1.50 for board and $1.50 a month for the hospital.[4]

Although the surveys made it apparent the town was in trouble, many aspects of life in St. Thomas continued on the way they had for the previous fifty years. Residents did not share the same dismal view of their agricultural prospects that H. L. Baldwin had, even though they recognized the necessity of improvements. To accommodate the need of agricultural expertise in southern Nevada, the Farm Bureau established a branch in St. Thomas. Keeping with the tradition of church leaders occupying positions of secular authority, Bishop Robert O. Gibson became president of the bureau.[5]

Sometimes, towns faced with a problem come up with rather odd solutions. Seizing upon the fact that the valley had experienced shortages of corn, farmers organized the Moapa Valley Corn Club. The club wanted to lay to rest the arguments of any skeptics who thought that corn would not grow in the valley. The club offered prizes for the best corn, poultry, and hogs. They accepted entries in three categories: local, statewide, and interstate. One of the members of the Corn Club was St. Thomas resident Berkeley Bunker, future US senator from Nevada.[6]

Despite a concerted effort to help the agricultural sector flourish, agriculturalists found it increasingly apparent in the 1920s that commercial farming was not a viable enterprise for St. Thomas. Residents still felt that it was a valuable area to grow grain, alfalfa, asparagus, carrots, turnips, cantaloupes, and other crops, but there was just not enough output to justify marketing facilities. They raised livestock but not in sufficient quantities for market, either. Even when marketable quantities were attempted, things just did not work out. Nellie Gentry decided to attempt to raise some pigs for market. She went to St. George and purchased two white pigs, bringing them back to St. Thomas in a Hudson car. She put them in the basement of a vacant house to raise them. They multiplied, and in two years the whole herd was ready for butchering. Before she was able to do that, the pigs contracted cholera and died.[7]

The rail spur that was so welcomed in 1912 required large amounts of products to justify sending cars to the end of the line. One farmer in St. Thomas found it necessary to haul his truck crops to Overton by automobile because he was not able to produce enough to permit car-lot shipment. Part of the problem St. Thomas faced is that the valley is narrow, and cantaloupes matured up to two weeks faster on the higher slopes than in the center of the valley. If their melons were to all ripen at the same time, they would have had enough to permit car-lot shipment. Even if that were the case, the railroad and refrigeration still ruined the market for St. Thomas melons. The melons in California's Imperial Valley ripened earlier and in much larger quantities, inundating the market before those from the Muddy Valley were ready for distribution.[8]

Major flooding that destroyed crops in 1920 and 1932 did not help the situation, either. Even if the floods were not catastrophic, they still did damage. Ruth Cornia remembered that one year they had a flood three Sundays in a row, covering their gardens, grapevines, fruit trees, and more. In an attempt to save the grapes, they waded out in the floodwater and picked them. They dipped the grapes in a weak lye solution and set them out to dry into raisins. Even that was a failure because flies got to them, and they had to be thrown out.[9]

The twenties were not uniformly bad for St. Thomas. The discovery of ancient Native American ruins focused the attention of many in the country on the town on the Lower Muddy. In 1924 excavation began on the Lost City-Anasazi ruins north of St. Thomas. There was great excitement among political leaders and scientists about the possibilities the ruins offered. Governor James Scrugham of Nevada recognized the site as a possible boon to tourism. Promoting the site, he said that "the most important contributions to archaeology ever found in the United States are being dug from the ruins of the buried city." Academics focused on the discovery that residents of the pueblo appeared to have developed their own written language. Even the local residents were excited about the Lost City. Mark R. Harrington of the National Museum of the American Indian in New York City superintended the excavation. He expressed his pleasure that the ranchers and residents to the Moapa Valley went out of their way to help the archaeological team perform their work.[10]

Residents had a good reason to be helpful. Any tourism to the area generated revenue. In national news, St. Thomas became associated with the Lost City. The *New York Times* and the *Los Angeles Times* carried stories about the discovery and what it meant for those interested in the early history of the Southwest. The *Los Angeles Times* story showed great excitement about the site. It read that it was "probably right here in the Moapa Valley that the ancestors of some of the modern Pueblo tribes learned how to build permanent dwellings, to weave fine cloth, to make good pottery, to practice agriculture— in brief, developed the arts which, in after days, made them one of the most highly civilized peoples in America north of Mexico." Another article said that a trip to the site was "perhaps the most interesting and historically significant motor-car trip that can be made." News of the discovery even found its way into the *Times* of London.[11]

To capitalize more fully on the tourist possibilities of the Lost City, Governor Scrugham conceived the idea of holding a pageant on the site. The theater department at Brigham Young University produced it. They brought in Native Americans from New Mexico and Arizona to augment the local Paiutes used in scenes. The pageant was a triumphalist narrative of the history of the valley. It showed the early residents of the Muddy working and playing at the Lost City, the ways of the Paiutes, and the travels of early explorers. It showed the arrival of the Mormon settlers and "civilization," the Mormon departure, and events up to the current day. The Union Pacific Railroad, one of the sponsors of the event, ran a special train to St. Thomas for the event. Approximately twenty-five hundred attended the pageant, the largest crowd ever assembled in the valley up to that date.[12]

Through the surveys and attention from the Lost City, St. Thomas seemed to continue to function as a community. The residents still knew how to throw a party as well. Their 1921 July 4 celebration was sufficiently spectacular to garner front-page attention from the *Las Vegas Age*. Reporter Dick Arnold said that the event brought in people from the entire Moapa Valley, including about one hundred Paiutes from the reservation. There were horse racing, auto racing, and rodeo events. The funds for the day's sports and barbecue came voluntarily from residents of St. Thomas. With the exception of the dance, the organizers charged nobody for participation.[13]

There were many positives for the town in the early twenties, but as the decade wore on, things began to unravel. The approach to the bridge over the Virgin River was washed out by a flood. This was not the first time it had happened, but it was the first time that it occurred when there was talk of putting the entire area under a reservoir. Because of the uncertainty and high costs associated with road construction in the area, the county commissioners decided to abandon the Arrowhead Trail route through St. Thomas. They routed the road through the Apex Summit, as the commissioners determined it would be a cheaper route to maintain.[14] Interstate 15 and Highway 93 today follow this new route.

The commission did not arrive at this decision lightly. In 1920 division engineer C. G. Benson of the Nevada Highway Department signed off on the highway continuing to go through St. Thomas because it would do the greatest good to the greatest number of people. The other route would bypass St. Thomas and Bunkerville on the way to Mesquite. The route through St. Thomas also promoted tourism in the Valley of Fire, which was a great asset to the area. Benson's report noted that on average, twenty-nine cars went through St. Thomas daily. The town was also already equipped to deal with tourist traffic. Roughly halfway between Los Angeles and Salt Lake City, St. Thomas offered shade, a hotel, good food, and a garage with experienced mechanics to keep cars running well. One of the businesses in town, the Arrowhead Store, catered to tourist traffic. It sold groceries and candies, had automobile service facilities, and operated a free campground. These assets made St. Thomas southern Nevada's "first widely publicized tourist arcadia," even if Rox Whitmore and Harry Gentry did have a regular income from pulling cars from the Virgin at two dollars apiece.[15]

Before making the determination, members of the Las Vegas Chamber of Commerce, the chairman of the Clark County Board of Commissioners, and the district engineer of the state highway commission went on a surveying expedition to explore the feasibility of the route change. After driving over the existing and proposed routes, they favored moving the road because the new shorter route would have fewer grades and cost less to construct. Another motivation for relocating the road was that Nevada could not

obtain any federal funds to repair the St. Thomas route because of the likelihood of the town's inundation.[16] Another factor may have been that in 1921,
copper prices dropped sharply and the Grand Gulch mine stopped shipping
ore through St. Thomas, so mining traffic had become a nonissue. After considering all the factors, the commissioners believed keeping the road on the
same route an untenable position.

St. Thomas residents were likely quite aware of the decision of the county
commission. Despite that knowledge, in March 1922, residents of St. Thomas
and Bunkerville raked forty miles of the Arrowhead Trail to make travel
over it more pleasant. This was a good decision, as relocating the road would
require a significant amount of time; meanwhile, it remained the only all-
weather automobile route between Salt Lake City and Los Angeles. Traffic
on the road continued to be good, as if "the entire east was moving west-
ward." In 1925, however, the good times came to an end. The bridge over
the Virgin at St. Thomas burned, and traffic was routed through Glendale
and Mesquite.[17] The move must have been very bitter for St. Thomas residents, considering that congressional approval for the dam required three
more years.

On December 21, 1928, President Calvin Coolidge signed the Boulder Canyon Project Act. Approval for the initial funding took until July 1930. Only
then did the government begin making real plans for relocating the 234
residents of St. Thomas and providing compensation for their lands that
would end up seventy feet under the surface of the water.[18] In order to do
that, the government required a detailed appraisal of the entire area. Secretary of the Interior Ray Lyman Wilbur began assembling an appraisal
board to complete the task. By September Cecil W. Creel, director of the
Agricultural Extension Division and professor of agricultural extension in
the College of Agriculture at the University of Nevada, Reno, received an
appointment as one of the appraisers, as did Harry Crain, an appraiser from
Cheyenne, Wyoming.

Creel suggested that the citizens of St. Thomas gather and elect one of
their own to serve on the appraisal board to protect their interests. During
this election, Levi Syphus received forty-eight out of fifty votes. Syphus, the
brother of Ellen Gentry, had served on the boards of several valley enter-
prises. The Nevada State Democratic Party leaders urged Syphus to run for
governor, but he declined because he felt the fact that he was both a Mormon and single would handicap him in a race. Tasker Oddie, US senator

from Nevada, wrote Secretary Wilbur to endorse Syphus. He indicated that he had known Syphus for many years and could "state unhesitatingly that he is a man of the highest honor, integrity, and ability, and I strongly recommend that he be appointed without further selection. . . . This will save unnecessary trouble and complications, and you will be perfectly safe in following this suggestion."[19] Wilbur followed the wishes of Senator Oddie and the residents of St. Thomas and appointed Syphus to serve on the board.

With the board assembled, the appraisal process was ready to proceed, but there was some disagreement on exactly how to do so. In December 1930, Harry Crain wrote Elwood Mead, secretary of the Bureau of Reclamation, indicating that he thought business deals in general would be better for both parties if concluded quickly. He recommended a quick survey and offer on land. To sweeten the deal for the landowners, the government would allow them to live on the land until the department needed it. The biggest problem with that approach, Crain explained, was that Cecil Creel had discovered that some people had bought tracts of land in the area to speculate on. Crain told Creel that this should not be a problem, because if they were ignored until the last moment, "we will be in a position to talk pretty straight to them."[20]

In Mead's reply, he agreed that it was usually the case that speedy business deals were most satisfactory, but not in this situation. Funds earmarked for purchasing land in the reservoir site drew 4 percent interest as long as the money stayed in government accounts, so there was no advantage to the government to purchase lands as quickly as possible, other than to conclude the matter. He agreed, however, that the best approach for dealing with recalcitrant landowners was to put them off as long as possible. He also approved of letting previous owners stay on the land after the sale, but with the caveat that the termination of lease agreements would occur before completion of the dam. Mead left the lease terms to the board to consider when affixing values to the land.

Secretary Mead underestimated the divisive potential of the survey. Crain expressed concern about the appraisers meeting resistance from landowners while they carried out the appraisal. Mead did not think that this should be a problem because the board would declare only the land's value, not negotiate the land purchases. It seems odd that he believed that just because the board would not be the ones handing out the money, they should encounter no significant resistance, yet that is what happened. Perhaps he was unconcerned because he did not think there would be much variation in land value from one tract to another. In a letter to W. W. Johnson, who apparently was an engineer for the Bureau of Reclamation, Mead requested that all private lands in the proposed reservoir be classified prior to appraisal, so the appraised price of each tract would be reasonably uniform, "as it should be between various tracts." That survey reported that there were 1,293.8 acres of cultivated land and 3,561.9 acres of uncultivated land, with four different categories of land values based on use.[21]

The government also needed to resolve the issue of the numerous mining claims surrounding St. Thomas. W. B. Acker, comptroller general of the United States, in a letter to the secretary of the interior, lamented that there were so many mining claims in the area, it would take almost twelve thousand dollars just to publish proceedings to take over the claims, which he did not have in his budget. There were a few valid claims that the government settled, but there were so many mining claims that were essentially worthless that the Bureau of Reclamation records were replete with copies of letters denying mining claims. The typical letter looked something like this:

> Sir or Madam: [depending on owner]
>
> By office letter __ of _____, adverse proceedings were directed against _____ mining claim in approximately Sec. ___ T.___ R. ___ upon the charges: 1. That the land within the limits of the claim is non-mineral in character. 2. That minerals in sufficient quantities have not been discovered within the limits of the claim to constitute a valid discovery. 3. That the mining location has been abandoned. . . . [T]he location is hereby declared null and void and the United States has taken possession of the land covered thereby for its own uses and purposes.
>
> The case is closed.[22]

Very few who received such letters contested the actions taken against their claims.

The appraisal of lands in and around St. Thomas did not go nearly so smoothly. The appraisal board quickly broke into two factions, with Levi Syphus fighting with Harry Crain and Cecil Creel. Being a resident of the town gave Syphus a different perspective on what had value, which was beyond what the market would bear, as he tried to explain to the others on the board. He wrote to Crain and Creel in April 1931:

The people have built themselves schools and churches, have established a communal and social life. All of these things have value and are to be completely destroyed. They cannot remain in the vicinity or enjoy the fruits of their past developments in these respects. The land is all taken and privately owned and the ousted settlers occupying the lands and towns to be flooded must move to an entirely new locality. As a consequence the benefits which the land enjoyed as being a part of the town and community center are items of value which should be considered. . . . Climate allows crops grown year round, two and sometimes three crops on same land in one year. For $6 an acre, phosphorous fertilizer vastly increases yield. Alfalfa yields over ten year period justify $800 an acre. Market price is not a fair way to judge value because the announcement of the dam stops people from wanting to buy the land. Even if it were not for that, there have not been enough recent sales to be able to judge what a fair price should be. It is an established precedent that owners of land are entitled to the value of the water right taken, even if they had not used that right. The agricultural survey shows underlying water, so land not under cultivation could be so used and should be paid for as such. There are numerous cases where the owners took the government to court and won, getting much more for their lands.

Syphus did recognize that as a member of the board, he was more than just a resident of St. Thomas, and he had to keep the best interests of the government in mind as well. He attempted to reconcile this by stating, "To the best of my knowledge and belief, lands generally elsewhere situate under like climatic condition to those of the Moapa Valley and having other similar favorable opportunities and conditions range higher in price than that at which I would evaluate the lands to be taken for Boulder Reservoir."[23] Crain and Creel were not moved by his logic.

While the appraisal board was wrangling over valuations, some of the residents of St. Thomas were getting restless and again enlisted Senator Oddie to contact the secretary of the interior on their behalf. Senator Oddie had some leverage beyond membership in the Senate. He, along with Reed Smoot, US senator from Utah and a Mormon, was a member of the Senate Appropriations Committee, which oversaw the Department of the Interior's budget. He also had friends in St. Thomas, friends who were anxious to know when the government would make them an offer for their homes and farms in the area to be covered by Lake Mead. Part of their anxiety came from the fact that they did not know if they should invest in new equipment and farm machinery needed to properly cultivate their farms. Oddie wrote, "It seems fair that these people should have some intimation as soon as possible as to when their lands will be taken over and paid for. Delay will cause them additional losses. In my opinion, this question should be decided with as little delay as possible."[24]

In the meantime, the Nevada Land and Livestock Company, which owned a large chunk of the lands in the reservoir site, requested a meeting with the appraisal board. They wanted to show their lands were especially valuable, not because of any agricultural output, but for becoming part of a reservoir that generated electrical power. They asked the board to consider this when they made valuations. While waiting for their meeting, company owners attempted to organize St. Thomas residents to bargain as a unit. J. R. Alexander, district council for the bureau, was concerned about the move, but realized that they could do nothing but let the effort "run its course."[25] Part of what Alexander was concerned about is that he conflated the owners of the Nevada Land and Livestock Company, many of whom were prominent church members, with the church itself. The church had greater resources to contest appraisals and offers than individual landowners did. The effort apparently "ran its course," as bureau records contain no more references to it.

The delay in making offers on land was the result not of any intransigence on the part of the Department of the Interior, but in reconciling the appraisals of the divided board. By August 1931, Elwood Mead was beginning to feel pressure from his superiors to expedite the completion of the appraisal. He felt that there was no hope of reconciling the different valuations, but if he and the chief engineer, Walker Young, did not move quickly, they would "have a good deal of explaining to do." He recommended that a majority and a minority report be filed and have Secretary Wilbur decide what course to take. Mead, however, recommended accepting the Crain and Creel valuations.[26]

The government finally published the appraisal report in October 1931. There were major differences between the majority report of Crain and Creel and Syphus's minority report. Part of that stemmed not just from the fact that Syphus was from the area, but from the methods that both sides used. Syphus merely assigned a value to each of the 266 tracts, whereas Crain and Creel attempted to justify their value estimates. They stated the land classification (agricultural, with or without water, in town, containing orchards, and so on) and what part of the total represented water rights or stock in the Muddy Valley Irrigation Company. The two reports agreed

TABLE 6.1
Summary of the Syphus appraisal

Total appraised price of land	$829,728.50
Total appraised price of improvements	131,430.25
TOTAL	$961,158.75

SOURCE: Walker R. Young and J. R. Alexander, Appraisal of Lands Which Will Be Flooded by Hoover Reservoir–Boulder Canyon Project (Department of the Interior, Bureau of Reclamation, October 7, 1931), 11.

TABLE 6.2
Summary of the Crain and Creel minimum appraisal

Acreage cultivated	1,509.15
Acreage uncultivated	6,517.72
Total acreage	8,026.90
[sic]	
Total number of tracts	218
Average size of tracts in acres	36.82
Total appraised price of land without water and improvements	$352,305.15
Average price per acre of land without water and improvements	$43.89
Total number of tracts with improvements	71
Total appraised price of improvements	$132,559.25
Average price per acre for improvements	$16.51
Estimated number of preferred shares of Muddy Valley Irrigation Co.	936.95
Estimated number of common shares of Muddy Valley Irrigation Co.	3,084.15
Total appraised price of shares of stock	$112,460.90
Estimated total appraised price of water	$115,999.90
Average price per acre for water rights	$14.45
Total appraised price of land with improvements and water	$600,864.30
Average price per acre of land with improvements and water	$74.85

SOURCE: Walker R. Young and J. R. Alexander, Appraisal of Lands Which Will Be Flooded by Hoover Reservoir–Boulder Canyon Project (Department of the Interior, Bureau of Reclamation, October 7, 1931), 8–11.

TABLE 6.3
Crain and Creel maximum appraisal

Total appraised price of land and water	$700,469.15
Total appraised price of improvements	132,559.25
TOTAL	$833,028.40

NOTE: The appraisal is basically an additional $100 per acre.

on 48 tracts, leaving 218 tracts in dispute. Syphus was generally more generous in his appraisals, but his valuations were actually lower on 20 tracts than Crain and Creel's. The tracts that the board agreed on covered 4,620.12 acres, all uncultivated. Only 21 tracts had water rights and were valued at $2.50 an acre; the rest were valued lower. The value of the tracts agreed upon was only $15,525, only 1–2 percent of the total value of land appraised.[27] The accompanying tables show the differences between the appraisals.

Predictably, the Bureau of Reclamation chose to follow Crain and Creel's minimum appraisal values, releasing their findings to the public and burying the minority report. The owners of each of the appraised tracts received letters advising them of how much the government was willing to pay for their land. There were many who owned land in the area who were disappointed when they did not receive an offer to purchase their lands. The Bureau of Reclamation fielded many letters from people offering their land for sale and requests to know if the government might need their land at some future date.

Newspapers throughout the West almost immediately began analyzing the offers and discussing what the offers meant for the residents of St. Thomas and Kaolin. Area ranchers were the first people notified of their land's appraised value. The *Las Vegas Review-Journal* reported that St. Thomas ranchers were to receive an average of $2,000, or slightly less than $40 an acre. The newspaper *Garfield County* of Panguitch, Utah, reported that approximately $500,000 was in store for landowners. As more information became available, the papers continued to follow the story. The August 4, 1932, edition of the *Review-Journal* listed the names, acreage, and prices for each of the tracts sold.[28] Certainly, part of why the appraisal values were front-page news in the region was that the country was in the midst of the Great Depression, and $2,000 would have been warmly welcomed by most Americans.

Since St. Thomas residents faced imminent dispossession from their homes, they exhibited understandable consternation over the appraisal's results. Many would likely have objected strenuously to their valuation even if Syphus had been able to dictate land prices. The bureau was able to resolve some of their concerns with relative ease. Many residents resented the fact that the government required title insurance, especially because if the government were to condemn the land, residents would have no guarantees that the title was free of defects. They requested that a current abstract of title showing no defects along with a deed be sufficient to allow the purchase to proceed, which the government accepted.[29]

Another shared issue was that Levi Syphus had been so obviously ignored as a member of the appraisal board. Richard Lyman, an LDS apostle who had written on behalf of St. Thomas residents, wrote to Elwood Mead that St. Thomas residents thought the bureau had an unfriendly attitude toward them. They believed the bureau opposed putting Syphus on the board but acceded because of outside pressure. Once he was on the board, he had very little influence on its decisions.[30]

The discussion between Walker Young and Elwood Mead on how to respond to Richard Lyman's letter is revealing. Young wrote:

> In discussing the matter of the ignoring of Mr. Syphus as one member of the Board of Appraisers we did not deem it advisable to state in the draft of [the] letter that we think that Mr. Syphus was more of an advocate than an appraiser and that in performing his services on the board we gained the impression that he was acting more as a agent of the land owners in getting as high prices as possible rather than as an impartial appraiser whose duty it was to be fair to the United States as well as the land owners.[31]

Though they would never admit it publicly, the bureau's attitude toward Syphus was exactly what Lyman and others believed. His appointment was a mere sop for the residents of St. Thomas and Kaolin.

Mr. Stewart wrote Elwood Mead asking for an explanation of the discrepancies between the majority and minority reports. He requested information on nine tracts. Young and Mead also discussed Stewart's letter. Their disgust with Syphus over this is apparent. Walker noted that he did not request information on three other tracts that he owned but upon which the full board agreed. The bureau never made the minority report public, so this information was available only from Syphus. Young wrote, "In this connection it will be remembered that Mr. Stewart under date of September 6, 1930 wrote a letter to the secretary, highly recommending Mr. Syphus as to his fitness as one of the appraisers and rather urging that he be appointed as such."[32]

Some of the disagreement over valuations arose because of cultural misunderstanding. Because St. Thomas was a farm village, residents valued the land in town more than farmland, regardless of water rights or productivity. Crain, though an appraiser, was not from an area that was predominantly Mormon. Creel's specialty was agriculture. Besides these factors, they were in a sense advising the government to offer a price that was reasonable for the rest of the country.

St. Thomas bishop Robert O. Gibson seemed confused by Crain and Creel's apparent ineptness, writing that what "hurt the people most is the great variation or inequality in the prices that have been fixed on property which actually has almost exactly the same *intrinsic* worth." Gibson was incredulous

TABLE 6.4
Minority and majority appraisal on selected tracts

Tract number	Syphus minority appraisal	Crain and Creel majority appraisal
124	$1,050	$200
170	400	200
217	5,430	2,025
227	250	300
228	750	750
229	1,980	750
230	600	225
231	3,060	1,075
232	660	250
TOTALS	$14,180	$5,775

SOURCE: "Memorandum, Subject: Appraisal of Tracts Belonging to Paul Stewart, et al.-Boulder Canyon Project, Construction Engineer (Walker R. Young) to Commissioner (Elwood Mead)," December 8, 1931, NARA, Denver, CO.

that the board would "place a valuation three times as great on areas which are down in the fields and cannot even be reached by alley ways, as they are placed on other areas located next to the principle streets in the city." For the Saints in St. Thomas, it seemed that the board arbitrarily paid high prices to some and low prices to others.[33]

Many of the objections raised came down to the fact that the government was requiring the people to give up their roots, their emotional investment in the land. No amount of money could satisfy them. The displaced lamented other intangibles. Walker Young recalled that John Perkins, who owned a house in St. Thomas, brought up the subject of the value of shade with the engineer. Young at first thought this was kind of a silly thing to worry about, but when he reflected upon it, he realized that shade was very valuable in St. Thomas and that "there wasn't anything on his place worth as much as that shade created by trees he'd planted years and years ago."[34]

Because so many strenuously objected to the assigned value that their land received, talk began to circulate about a possible reappraisal. Walker Young and J. R. Alexander considered the possibility in their analysis of the newly completed appraisal. They felt that the poor lands appraised at $2.50 an acre received the proper appraisal as for use value, but the price was so small it might force the government to condemn the land. The small offers left landowners with little to lose over challenging the valuation in court. They worried there was little likelihood that a jury would award less than $2.50 and would likely award more. If challengers received more, it would create discontent with those who settled for the lower price. One bureau official, Pr. Walker, suggested raising the minimum price per acre to $5.00, but worried that those who owned lands that were more valuable would want their prices raised proportionally as well.[35]

Walker Young broached the subject with J. R. Alexander, district council, and Elwood Mead in early December 1931. They desired not to publish the appraised values, but a demand from the Bank of Pioche for the valuations on some of their properties forced publication.[36] The resurvey effort seemed to gain some steam, as the dissatisfied landowners hired the St. George law firm of Clark, Richards, and Bowen to represent them.

Elwood Mead was firm in his refusal to consider revisiting the appraisal. In a letter to Senator Oddie, Mead wrote that he reviewed all the records of the appraisal, and everything seemed in order. He expressed the opinion that the lawyers representing the landowners were little more than opportunistic rabble-rousers whose arguments were largely without merit. Mead said the values assigned seemed liberal at the time and were far more generous in light of the valley's current agricultural condition.[37] Mead minced no words with apostle Richard Lyman. Mead wrote, "If people had a problem with the appraisal, they would need to challenge it in the courts." He said that Lyman did not realize the "friendly spirit" that prompted appraising the land years before it was actually needed. If residents did not like the appraisal, they were free to reject the offer. Further, he wrote that holding out for the value listed in the minority report was ill-advised, because its valuations "were so far out of line with prices being paid for farm property elsewhere that there seemed to be no economic justifications of its values."[38]

Mead's arguments did not satisfy those who were unhappy with the assigned value of their land, but Mead was at least able to quash talk of opening up the appraisal again. It was clear that "there was nothing to argue," said William Murphy, who was born and raised in St. Thomas. "The government said, 'Move out or we're going to flood you.'"[39]

The town had begun to die when state engineers rerouted the highway through Apex. The demise began in earnest once the appraisal was finished and the government began sending notices to owners. Staying was not an option, so the soon-to-be-displaced began looking for places to go and establish new homes before their temporary leases on their previous homes ran out. Some tore down their homes and rebuilt them at Overton, Alamo, or Nepae, a Y on the railroad only a short distance north of St. Thomas but above the projected shoreline.[40] A group of people went to Mount Trumbull on the Arizona Strip.

Reminiscent of the first abandonment of St. Thomas, some discussed relocating the entire town to another location. One of the proposed sites lay in the Pahranagat Valley on the ten-thousand-acre Greer Wright Ranch. The ranch included water rights from Crystal Springs and Ash Springs, the combined flow of them being enough to irrigate the land. Tellingly, not much of the area was under cultivation at the time, but was used as range for cattle. The owner lived in South America and proposed cutting up the acreage into one-hundred-acre lots for Mormon truck farmers.[41]

The other idea advanced for keeping the community intact in another location was moving St. Thomas residents to the Pahrump Valley. In April 1932, unidentified "Salt Lake leaders" inspected the Pahrump Ranch, owned by the Southern Pacific Railroad. The twelve-thousand-acre ranch, though fertile, was 135 miles away from St. Thomas and in the middle of nowhere.[42] It is not clear if the people from Salt Lake did not close the deal or if St. Thomas residents refused to be involved, but the plan did not come to fruition.

News of the proposed move to Pahrump reached Harry Crain. Evidently, Crain harbored some bitterness over the appraisal process in the Moapa Valley, because his comments on the notion are acidic, as in this letter to Elwood Mead:

> My dear Doctor Mead
>
> I am enclosing herewith a clipping from the Denver Post. I think with a little bit of study and a little bit of thought you can read between the lines of this scheme. I am willing to bet a dollar to a doughnut that this is a deal which is being fostered by the Richards and Brown people of Salt Lake City. It looks to me that they are having a rather poor luck in fleecing the poor, poverty stricken Mormons in the Moapa Valley, and are now resorting to this method to get another whack at the little bunch of money that they are destined to get from the government for their holdings in the vicinity of St. Thomas.[43]

Regardless of where they went, many of the departing residents left with great heaviness in their hearts. Vivian Frehner remembered that when he and his family left St. Thomas, he kicked the wall of their house on his last trip out the door. His mother heard the blow and came running. Vivian defensively stated that they were going to tear the house down in the morning.

His mother said, "That doesn't make any difference to me, I want that home the way it was."[44]

The government announced the results of the appraisal in October 1931. St. Thomas became a ghost town less than a year later. Apostle Richard Lyman, in one of his letters to Elwood Mead, related Robert O. Gibson's sad report of the condition of the town. While discussing the situation in St. Thomas as both were attending the General Conference, Lyman directed Bishop Gibson to advise members of the St. Thomas Ward to remain on their land until the government really needed the land and made an offer on it. Gibson replied that the community had been wrecked. Half the population had moved. The school had lost two of its three teachers, and church organizations were nearly paralyzed. "Remaining," Bishop Gibson said, "in a community as badly wrecked as St. Thomas is wrecked is extremely undesirable and unpleasant and well-nigh impossible."[45] The town was still six years from going under the water of the lake named after the man Lyman appealed to, yet the dam had already killed St. Thomas.

The Roaring Twenties did not roar for St. Thomas. Mining left the area, the county relocated the highway, the railroad began cutting back trips there, the survey of the Colorado proceeded, and a short distance into the next decade saw the town bought out and largely abandoned. Those who remained began quietly marking time, waiting for the water to reach them in their homes. The demise of the town could have been the subject of the T. S. Eliot poem "The Hollow Men," going out "not with a bang but a whimper."[46]

7

Coup de Grace?

St. Thomas resident Hugh Lord did not believe that the waters of Lake Mead would ever actually reach St. Thomas. Early in June 1938, Lord went fishing, driving his car down the Muddy Valley and parking about one hundred yards from the water on a gentle slope. He had some success fishing, spending several hours out of sight of his car. About nightfall, he decided to pack up and go home. He went to where he thought he had parked his car, but it was gone. Looking out into the water, he discovered his car with the water swirling around his running boards. Driving back to St. Thomas, he began to reconsider his position on leaving.

We have previously discussed the decree of death for St. Thomas. Now, its execution: the disbanding of their ward, the salvage of buildings and the railroad, as well as ongoing legal battles over land valuation. Plans for Lake Mead killed St. Thomas, but it took several years before the reservoir filled and delivered the finishing blow. As journalist Jori Provas later described it, "St. Thomas did not die. It was murdered. Not maliciously, but definitely with aforethought. St. Thomas was surrendered, given up, sacrificed, if you will, for the good of the many."[1] For some, their suffering was greater because the element of surprise was absent. They could sit and watch the water inexorably engulf their beloved homes.

Before the water arrived, there were things that needed to be done. One took place on May 14, 1933, when the St. Thomas Ward, which had once recovered from virtual extinction, permanently disbanded. The program for the meeting called for that purpose included Bunker, Syphus, and other significant area names. At the end of the meeting, the members present raised their right hands to consent to the dissolution of the ward.[2] Many tears fell as the meeting ended and people returned to the business of leaving.

Other more mundane, earthly matters required attention before water came as well. Valley residents and Civilian Conservation Corps workers of the Overton camp cut down trees. A few of those who stayed leased farmland from the government and grew crops up through 1937. Nevertheless, by 1935 the town was a virtual ghost town, leaving only a handful of people who believed that the water would not actually ever reach them.[3]

As St. Thomas residents evacuated, it was not just the living that made good their escape. In 1934 the government began preparations to move the cemetery in St. Thomas, as well as smaller burial grounds in Kaolin and Rioville. Although the federal government moved the bodies, it still needed permission from Clark County to open the graves and transport them. After obtaining permission in late December, the government's mortician, Howell C. Garrison of Boulder City, moved the few bodies in Rioville, being the closest to the Colorado and subject to inundation earlier. Garrison moved the St. Thomas and Kaolin cemeteries in February and March 1935. The last graves, including Harry Gentry's and Ellen Gentry's, arrived at their new final resting place on March 4. The most recent grave belonged to June Syphus, who had died in Las Vegas in 1931.[4]

Completion of Hoover Dam in 1935 began the final deathwatch of the town. One front page of the *Las Vegas Review-Journal* stated that Lake Mead's waters were "only" sixteen miles away from St. Thomas. Another front-page article a year later reported that the town would remain dry for at least another year since the water level was seventy-eight feet below the contour that would begin the flooding of the site. In 1937 twelve miles separated the water from the town, and the fields were still in use to grow crops.[5] The railroad, whose arrival was heralded in 1912, was taken up by crews to save the valuable rails from the lake. In June 1938, the clock for St. Thomas ran out.

Bureau of Reclamation engineers watched the water rise with great attentiveness. Recognizing the interest the public had in the story, they estimated the town's submergence as June 17, 1938.[6] Heavier than expected runoff from snowfall in the Rockies made it clear that the town would not make it that long. The last few holdouts finally admitted that the flooding was going to happen.

John Perkins, one of those who believed the water would never reach the town, spent several days trying to save as much as possible from the houses he bought from the government for salvage. By June 8, Perkins realized that he would not have time to save at least three or four residences he had planned to raze or move elsewhere.[7] About the same time, St. Thomas resident Hugh Lord contemplated the rising water on a fishing trip and rethought his wager against the arrival of the water.

Arriving back in town, he sought out his friend and fellow holdout Rox Whitmore and told him that the time had probably come for them to leave. Despite the fact that he once gave ten-to-one odds that the water would not come, he spent the next several days getting every worker he could lay hands on to help him move his shop and vehicles to higher ground.[8] On June 11, Lord awoke to water swirling around his bed. The day to leave had come. Loading his last few possessions into a rowboat, he lit his house on fire and rowed away.

Lord, Whitmore, and Perkins were not the only ones forced out by rising waters. Frank Guetzill stayed with his herd of burros. The Bunker brothers, Brian, Berkeley, Wendell, Martin, and Vernon, all left on the last day of the town's existence, though they had already moved their belongings to Las Vegas. Berkeley Bunker later served as a US senator from Nevada. Interest in the event was so keen, one reporter considered the fact that two of the holdouts were abandoned dogs newsworthy enough to warrant a front-page story in the *Review Journal*.[9]

Leland "Rox" or "Rock" Whitmore and his wife were the only other holdouts. Whitmore was the postmaster and spent the last day of the town's existence busily canceling letters and postcards. In June 1935, stamp collector H. D. Sterling made note of editorials in several newspapers saying that St. Thomas was going under the water soon. Because last-day covers are valuable to stamp collectors, he hatched a plan. He designed a postcard showing the town going under and placed ads in philatelic papers and magazines, announcing the last-day covers. Within a few days, Sterling's mailbox overflowed with dimes, quarters, checks, dollar bills, money orders, and requests for credit. He carefully made out the orders to wait for the last-day stamp and sent them to St. Thomas for a long vacation. When the town did not go under that year, more orders poured in.

Sterling began receiving mail of a different sort. One said, "I want my 'ghost town' covers. If you can't deliver at once, then send my dime back."

Another read, "I sent you one dollar for covers from the Nevada ghost town. . . . [W]here are they? Either send me the covers or my dollar. The government takes care of cases such as yours." By June 1936, Sterling answered 240 letters and refunded twenty-three dollars. The next year the letters got even angrier. "My little boy sent you a dime for a ghost town or submarine cover and he didn't get either. I am going to report your activities to the post office department." "You send my half dollar back or you'll be up there with the rest of the fish. You can't stall me any longer. The dam is full of water and I know St. Thomas is under water." Refund or no refund, the letters stayed in St. Thomas, where some of them ended up being chewed on by mice who had taken up residence in the post office. Sterling must have been mightily relieved when the day to cancel the mail that had been waiting for three years finally came.[10]

Sterling may have been happy, but it must have been a daunting task for the postmaster and his wife. They spent the entire day canceling nearly five thousand postcards and letters sent them by Sterling and other philatelists around the world. When they finished, they had to wade with the mailbags to their waiting vehicle to take the mail up the valley. To put a note of finality on the affair, Whitmore threw the canceling stamp out into the advancing waters of Lake Mead.[11]

When the sun rose on the Moapa Valley on June 12, it did not rise on St. Thomas, buried by water and progress; the town was no more. In the seventy-three years of the town's existence, it died twice. This time, however, it appeared permanent. The death was made even harsher for some by the fact that they still held legal title to land now under water. The next several years saw legal wrangling that refused to let St. Thomas rest in peace.

Landowners George E. Knauth, John F. Perkins, W. H. Ensign, T. M. Farrand, and Leslie R. Saunders of the Nevada Land and Livestock Company, among others, flatly refused to accept the valuations assigned by the survey. The matter was still unresolved in the summer of 1943, when William E. Warne, commissioner of the Bureau of Reclamation, wrote to the chief engineer in Denver that the time had probably come to commence condemnation proceedings. The landowners made it apparent they were not going to settle for what the government was willing to offer. The government avoided this step before because of the likelihood that the cost of litigation would exceed the value of the land. Nevertheless, Warne felt that "the Government probably would be money ahead when one considers the time that has been

consumed, and the time that will be consumed in the future, in unsuccessful negotiations." Warne therefore requested that if he, the chief engineer,
agreed, Warne would instruct the director of power to notify the owners
that unless they accepted the appraised prices, condemnation proceedings
would begin.[12]

District council Richard Coffey responded to Warne that there was no
need to begin condemnation proceedings. The thirty unresolved tracts were
valued at only $6,489.70, with the most valuable one being $750. Coffey fig-
ured that the cost of condemnation proceedings against all the tracts would
far exceed the value of the land. More important, Coffey stated, was that he
was reluctant to cause the landowners any expense litigation would inevita-
bly bring. Instead, those unwilling to accept the appraised price were welcome to file suit under the Tucker Act in district court. Looking at some of
the tracts, it is clear why the bureau took this position. For example, tract
180, owned by George E. Knauth, was valued at only $100. Only 50 percent of
the tract would ever be under the water, even when Lake Mead reached full
capacity. At the time of Coffey's letter, no water had even reached it.[13]

The landowners received letters advising them of the bureau's continued
determination to use the official appraisal to guide compensation issues.
Walker Young wrote to the commissioner explaining why he felt that the
letters were a waste of ink and postage. The bureau sent W. H. Ensign letters in 1934 and 1939 seeking a resolution. Ensign's reply to the 1939 letter
read, "Why the people as a whole should take from one member at less than
cost—as a policy of the present Administration—is too Nazi for me—for my
ancestors helped in making the original U.S. Constitution." This language is
clearly coming from someone who was definitely not ready to settle.

The correspondence with John Perkins was more substantial, but no
less firm. The twelve letters in Perkins's file all center on his dissatisfaction
with the price established by Crain and Creel and the government's failure
to find evidence that the price of $150 was unjust. Perkins wanted $500. A
Mr. Littler, who worked in Young's office, contacted Perkins several times
in 1942 on other matters, and each time asked when Perkins was going to
sell his tract to the government. At every instance, Perkins replied, "When
they decide to give me $500 for it." Young saw no other possible resolution
besides condemnation.[14]

By 1945, eight years after the town went under and fourteen after the pub-
lishing of the appraisal, the government grew tired of waiting. E. A. Moritz,

Bureau of Reclamation acting regional director, decided that there was no reasonable prospect of obtaining the tracts belonging to Saunders and the Nevada Land and Livestock Company at a price satisfactory to the government and recommended condemnation proceedings. This time the regional director approved condemnation, and the attorney general filed a Declaration of Taking, paying Saunders $2,028.45 for his land.[15] Available Bureau of Reclamation records are silent on the disposition of the other contested tracts, but similar treatment to Saunders is likely. St. Thomas could now rest in peace, at least for a while.

Sodden Phoenix

St. Thomas was scarcely under the water when people began looking anxiously forward to the time when it would emerge from the depths.
Fluctuations in water levels have exposed the town site several times. This
chapter recounts these emergences and the reunions of former residents
held when that happened. It also discusses the town's subsequent loss of
identity. As it emerged from the water in 1999, possibly for the last time, the
site has prompted questions about conservation, recreation, and the future
of water in the region.

St. Thomas was finally legally laid to rest at the same time lower than average snowfall in the mountains allowed the town to emerge from the murky
depths in 1945. Like gawkers around the scene of an accident, people began to
flock to the town site to see what remained. Papers encouraged the pilgrimage with headlines like "St. Thomas Up from Watery Grave" and "Remember
St. Thomas? Here 'Tis Again, Back from Depths of Mead."[1] The second head-
line blazed over a full-page spread of pictures in the *Las Vegas Review-Journal*.

The foundations emerged from the water again in 1946 and 1947. By this
time, the remains of St. Thomas became a tourist attraction. Behind the
remains of Hugh Lord's garage were the remains of three Model Ts and a
1913 Cadillac, and many people were photographed sitting in them. Others
used their film to document fishing off foundations, climbing dead trees,
and looking for lost treasures. One of these treasures included the canceling
stamp thrown into the water by Whitmore. The stamp is now in possession
of an area resident.

For some, visits to the site became an amusing yearly ritual. A tone of disappointment permeated Ed Oncken's report to his readers in 1948 that the town was not going to make an appearance that year. In addition to making occasional appearances from the depths, St. Thomas made the news again in 1951 when the county commissioners decided that the time had finally come to repeal the ordinance that prohibited animals from running free on its streets.[2] Apparently, fish were free to roam.

When St. Thomas emerged from the water in the 1940s, those who came to visit were old residents and the curious, but there was nothing organized about their visits. When the town resurfaced again in 1952, former residents organized a reunion. They held it around the foundation of the old schoolhouse. In the midst of the program, a young boy exploring a cistern fell in, interrupting the program as reminiscing gave way to rescuing. The cistern was only half full, but about six feet down to the water, the walls were vertical, and there was only a small opening at the top. Rescuers lowered another boy down through the opening headfirst, and the boy who had been treading water grabbed the other boy's arms. Rescuers then pulled both boys out of the hole. The reporter from the *Review Journal* covering the reunion did not report the cistern incident, but did say that a good percentage of the population of southern Nevada was born or lived at one time in St. Thomas.[3] The article contains no clue as to what percentage they considered to be "good."

The opportunity for another reunion of former residents of St. Thomas arose in late 1964.[4] As chance would have it, low water enabled those interested in attending the one-hundred-year anniversary party of the arrival of Thomas S. Smith's party on the Muddy and the establishment of the town to do so on location. This was the last major gathering of former residents.

Several influential people from the town and surrounding area spoke at the reunion and shared stories about the good times they had in St. Thomas. A Mr. Perkins, who lived in Overton, said that there were some very beautiful girls in the town, and he "pursued some of the[m] very diligently." At the end of one visit, Perkins recalled, he stole a horse in St. Thomas in order to get back to Overton. The owner, carrying a 30.30 rifle, pursued him. Perkins escaped and later obtained forgiveness from the man, presumably after returning the horse.[5]

Former senator Berkeley L. Bunker, who was wearing an extremely beat-up hat, also spoke. Bunker claimed that he buried the hat by his house when he was forced from the valley by rising waters. When he arrived that morning at the reunion, he dug it up and put it on. He also proceeded to speak of all the good times he had in St. Thomas.[6] Rather than lamenting the decision of the government to destroy the town, the reunion focused on the good grounding and wonderful times that those who had lived there enjoyed. The remnants of St. Thomas, according to those assembled, belonged fully to former residents and their descendants. This is not to say that they bristled at the presence of outsiders, but rather that they did not seem to think anyone else was interested. In the twentieth century, this attitude prevailed every time water levels dropped enough for foundations to emerge.

A new century brought a new attitude toward the defunct town. Lake Mead hit an all-time high-water mark in 1983. In the late 1990s, the US West entered a drought. In 2002, five years into the drought, St. Thomas began to emerge once more from the depths. Very few people who lived in the town are alive today, and their descendants have no significant direct experience with the place. This left St. Thomas without a clear identity. John L. Smith asked the question in 2003, "Why was lowly, mud-caked St. Thomas so important, and what can we still learn from it?"[7] What is the story of this sodden phoenix, which seems to continually rise from the ruins of its former selves?

The National Park Service, which administers the site of St. Thomas, has taken the question posed by Smith very seriously. One of the reasons is their directive to interact with the public in a practice they call "civic engagement." Civic engagement, according to the Park Service, is "a continuous, dynamic conversation with the public on many levels that reinforces public commitment to the preservation of heritage resources, both cultural and natural, and strengthens public understanding of the full meaning and contemporary relevance of these resources."[8] Historic interpretation is to be a collaborative process with the National Park Service and American society.

One of the issues that the public was concerned about was the sudden influx of treasure hunters to St. Thomas once word got out that it had emerged from the water. Area resident John L. Smith expressed anger about this. He wrote, "What compelling artifacts there might have been, according to published reports, probably were plucked by the curious not long after word spread that the ghost of St. Thomas was reappearing at the lakeside. That's a shame. In a place where history is more cherished, such a sighting might have provided a chance for university graduate students to descend and begin excavation and cataloging of remnants of Nevada's past. But

Southern Nevada has been much too busy growing to care much about preserving its beginnings."[9]

The treasure hunting is justified by some who claim that the government dug up and took whatever artifacts it wanted in the 1920s, referring to the Lost City, so everything else is fair game. St. Thomas is in a recreation area, and some people want to dig things up in the name of recreation. This attitude made Darrell Wade of Mesquite livid. He challenged those who felt that way to extend their logic to a Native American site or a cemetery. Wade was emphatic that the town belonged to everyone and deserved protection so that everyone had the chance to enjoy it.[10]

The Park Service agreed with Wade, as his opinion mirrored established policy, and moved to make policies on how to deal with this specific site and determine which artifacts qualified as historically significant. To protect the site, the Park Service had to ban overnight camping near St. Thomas. Scavengers descended on the town at night with metal detectors in search of old railroad ties and auto parts. Greed motivated some, who heard a rumor that a five-dollar gold piece had been unearthed there. Rangers arrested more than a dozen people in 2004 for taking items from the protected area.[11]

Public historians also use the term *civic engagement* to describe the process of drawing in the public to interact with a site on a personal level. A gathering of historic-site directors explained, "We hold in common the belief that it is the obligation of historic sites to assist the public in drawing connections between the history of our sites and its contemporary implications." The challenge, then, of civic engagement is to make the transition from "representing history from singular perspectives to being centers for dialogue about how we can use history to build a better future."[12] The public has begun to do this with St. Thomas.

One of the most basic ways the public engages with St. Thomas today is through recreation. The St. Thomas Loop is a well-hiked trail. St. Thomas is an easily accessible ghost town relatively close to Las Vegas and has been the site of many formal and informal hiking excursions. For the recreation minded, it provides another interesting destination to participate in recreation and learn at the same time.[13]

St. Thomas also serves as a center for dialogue about water in southern Nevada. A few months after the water dropped enough to expose the concrete remnants of the town, John Smith said that the submergence of the town in 1938 was a symbol of the modern world of prosperity and plenty. Its reemergence reminds us of the fragility of life in Nevada: "Booms will bust, the most important oasis might one day be forgotten, the richest claims eventually play out, and water is never in great abundance in the desert." When the Scripps Institution of Oceanography announced that Lake Mead, if current use patterns continue, could go dry in thirteen years, St. Thomas again served as a cautionary tale for southern Nevada and the use of water.[14] This is very different from the "grow where you are planted" attitude the original inhabitants had for the town. Although weather patterns certainly can change and submerge the town once again, muting its current significance as a "cautionary tale," its history will serve the same purpose.

Regardless of the meanings St. Thomas holds for the individual reader, the town is clearly significant in the history of southern Nevada. The site was at one time considered a better place to settle than Las Vegas and ended up being one of the largest and most important towns in the area. It tells of how people's lives are affected when the government moves borders and takes land, but also of the determination of those left behind to make things work. It is the story of small-town America at the beginning of the modern era and a reflection of how water and the federal government intersect in the West. Ordinary citizens, senators, and criminals all rested their heads there, as is appropriate for a town that, by virtue of being in a national recreation area, belongs to us all. St. Thomas, for being in the middle of nowhere, was certainly at the center of things.

Notes

Introduction

1. http://www.snwa.com/html/drought_index.html; John L. Smith, "Town's Ruins Emerge from Water to Whisper," *Las Vegas Review-Journal*, February 20, 2003, B1.

2. Edward E. Baldwin, "Las Vegas in Popular Culture"; Hal Rothman, *Neon Metropolis: How Las Vegas Shed Its Stigma and Became the First City of the Twenty-First Century*.

1 · Physical Setting, Native American Usage, and Pre-Muddy Mission Mormon Movement

1. S. George Ellsworth, *Samuel Claridge: Pioneering the Outposts of Zion*, 81, 87. The original is a memoir in the article "From an Adobe Hut to a Mansion of Brick and Stone," *Deseret Evening News*, June 6, 1903.

2. Leroy R. Hafen and Ann W. Hafen, *Journals of Forty-Niners: Salt Lake to Los Angeles*, 87.

3. *Journal History of the Church of Jesus Christ of Latter-day Saints* (December 31, 1849). The *Journal History* is a massive collection of clippings, articles, and primary source documents relating to church history maintained by the Church Historical Department. The collection is indexed by day that the reported events occur.

4. George W. Brimhall, *The Workers of Utah*, 41.

5. W. Paul Reeve, *Making Space on the Western Frontier: Mormons, Miners, and Southern Paiutes*, 10–14.

6. "See an Ancient Sloth's Bones Dug Out of Gypsum Cave," *Millard County Chronicle*, January 29, 1931.

7. Michael R. Harrington, "A Primitive Pueblo City in Nevada," 262–77.

8. Parley P. Pratt autobiography, 378, 406, as quoted in Andrew Karl Larson, "Agricultural Pioneering in the Virgin River Basin," 40; Hafen and Hafen, *Journals of Forty-Niners*, 87.

9. Larson, "Agricultural Pioneering," 33–34; Leroy R. Hafen and Ana W. Hafen, *The Old Spanish Trail*, 323–24.

10. John C. Frémont, *Memoirs of My Life*, 378–80, as quoted in Larson, "Agricultural Pioneering," 37.

11. Richard E. Gillies, "A History of Lincoln County, Nevada, 1776–1874," 13.

12. Clifford Dale Harrison, *The Ashley-Smith Explorations*, 187; Hafen and Hafen, *The Old Spanish Trail*, 113–14.

13. Scholars of Mormon history, LDS and non-LDS alike, often refer to members of the Church of Jesus Christ of Latter-day Saints simply as "Saints." The term *Mormon* was originally a pejorative used to illustrate the belief that a Mormon was not a Christian. The use of the term *Saint* allows writers to refer to members of the LDS

Church quickly and easily and is in no way indicative of the idea that everyone who is not a Saint is naturally a sinner.

14. Starr Pearson Corbett, "A History of the Muddy Mission," 17–18.

15. Allan Nevins, *Fremont, the West's Greatest Adventurer*, 202–3.

16. John Charles Frémont, *Report of the Exploring Expedition to the Rocky Mountains in the Year 1842, and to Oregon and California in the Years 1843–44*, 379–80.

17. *The Diary of Orville C. Pratt*, as quoted in Hafen and Hafen, *The Old Spanish Trail*, 324–25.

18. Hafen and Hafen, *The Old Spanish Trail*, 314.

19. Martha C. Knack, *Boundaries Between: The Southern Paiute, 1775–1995*, 10–29.

20. James H. McClintock, *Mormon Settlements in Arizona*, 102.

21. Melvin T. Smith, "The Lower Colorado River: Its History in the Lower Canyons Area," 26, 35.

22. Gillies, "History of Lincoln County," 24.

23. *Journal History* (March 21, 1870), 2.

24. Brigham Young to John Eldridge, March 14, 1854, Brigham Young letterpress copybook, Box 1, Folder 6.

25. Knack, *Boundaries Between*, 54.

26. *Deseret News*, June 15, 1858.

27. Young to Major George W. Armstrong, Indian agent, February 9, 1856, Young letterpress copybook, Box 16, Folder 2.

28. The Mormons viewed themselves as the Lord's chosen people, a modern-day Israel. Just as in the Old Testament, those who were not part of Israel were Gentiles. It was extremely common for early Latter-day Saints to refer to any non-Mormons as Gentiles. The term was not necessarily a negative one.

29. Young to Amasa Lyman, July 18, 1854, Young letterpress copybook, Box 2, Folder 1.

30. Andrew Jensen, ed., "History of the Las Vegas Mission," 201–2.

31. Young to William Bringhurst, September 30, 1856, Young letterpress copybook, Box 3, Folder 5.

32. Young to Miles Anderson, October 4, 1856, ibid.

33. Gillies, "History of Lincoln County," 34–35.

34. *Deseret* was the Saints' word for the honeybee, which, along with the hive, symbolized industry and hard work.

35. James G. Bleak, *Annals of the Southern Utah Mission*, August 1857.

36. "Manuscript Histories of the Church: The Muddy Mission."

37. Bleak, *Annals*, January 1858.

38. *Journal History* (October 19, 1862).

39. Bleak, *Annals*, August 5, 1865. Panaca was in Utah at the time, though it is now in Nevada.

40. John M. Townley, *Conquered Provinces: Nevada Moves Southeast, 1864–1871*, 8, 10–11.

41. Young to the bishops and the brethren, January 3, 1865, Young letterpress copybook, Box 8, Folder 3.

42. Brimhall, *The Workers of Utah*, 41.

43. Young to Jacob Hamblin, February 4, 1864, Young letterpress copybook, Box 8, Folder 3; M. Smith, "Lower Colorado River," 230–31.

44. Elder Jeffrey R. Holland, address at Nevada Stake Conference broadcast, March 4, 2007, transcript in possession of the author; James H. Wood, "William Wood on the Muddy Valley Mission, 1867–72"; Bleak, *Annals*, May 2, 1869.

45. *Journal History* (November 10, 1864).

46. Young to Daniel H. Wells and Brigham Young Jr., November 18, 1864, Young letterpress copybook, Box 8, Folder 2; Young to Judge J. F. Kinney, December 23, 1864, ibid.

47. Bleak, *Annals*, December 17, 1864.

48. Ibid., October 7, 1864, April 26, 1865.

49. *Journal History* (November 10, 1864), and Young to Hy. W. Miller, November 8, 1864, Young letterpress copybook, Box 8, Folder 3.

50. Wood, "William Wood."

2 · *Establishing an Outpost of Zion*

1. Arabell Lee Hafner, *100 Years on the Muddy*, 27; *Journal History*, 2n12. There was a Ute near Provo who was also referred to as "Old Bishop" because of his resemblance to a local bishop. The record is silent on whether this was the case with the Paiute "Old Bishop."

2. Ramona Wilcox Cannon, "Aunt Hannah Sharp and the Muddy Mission."

3. Wood, "William Wood"; Hafner, *100 Years on the Muddy*, 72.

4. "Mrs. Elizabeth Claridge McCune."

5. D. W. Meinig, "The Mormon Culture Region: Strategies and Patterns in the Geography of the American West, 1847–1964," 198; Wallace Stegner, *Mormon Country*, 28.

6. Richard H. Jackson, "The Mormon Village: Genesis and Antecedents of the City of Zion Plan," 223; Young to Joseph S. Murdock, March 11, 1868, Young letterpress copybook, Box 10, Folder 5.

7. Ronald W. Walker, "Golden Memories: Remembering Life in a Mormon Village," 212.

8. Joseph Smith Jr., *History of the Church of Jesus Christ of Latter-day Saints*, 3:56; Meinig, "Mormon Culture Region," 198; Lowry Nelson, *The Mormon Village: A Pattern and Technique of Land Settlement*, 52–53.

9. As quoted in Neil R. Peirce, *The Mountain States of America: People, Politics, and Power in the Eight Rocky Mountain States*, 187; George Q. Cannon, ed., *Journal of Discourses*, 16:143–44.

10. *Journal History* (January 12, 1865); *Acts, Resolutions, and Memorials, Passed and Adopted by the Legislative Assembly of the Territory of Utah*, 14th sess., January 11, 1865.

11. Bleak, *Annals*, May 24, 1865; "Manuscript Histories of the Church"; Record of Baptisms, 1866–67, Moapa Stake Records.

12. Ipson Family Papers.

13. US Bureau of the Census, "Manuscript Census of the Territory of Utah," Rio Virgin County, 1870, as quoted in S. George Ellsworth, *Mormon Settlement on the Muddy*, 12.

14. M. Smith, "Lower Colorado River," 309. The October 6, 1867, entry in Bleak's *Annals* lists the names of all 158 called during that conference. Other sources list the number called as 163. Young to John Brown, October 18, 1867, and Young to Franklin D. Richards, October 18, 1867, Young letterpress copybook, Box 10, Folder 3; R. Cannon, "Aunt Hannah Sharp."

15. *Journal History* (April 15, 1868); Young to Geo. Nebeker, November 21, 1868; Young to Heber Young, October 22, 1868; Young to A. Carrington, January 5, 1869, Young letterpress copybook, Box 11, Folders 2–3.

16. Bleak, *Annals*, November 1, 1866, April 10, 1867; M. Smith, "Lower Colorado River," 173.

17. John W. Powell, *The Exploration of the Colorado River and Its Canyons*, 286; William Culp Darrah, "George Y. Bradley's Journal, May 24–August 30, 1869," 31–72.

18. Powell, *Exploration of the Colorado River*, 286; Frederick S. Dellenbaugh, *A Canyon Voyage*, 174–75.

19. Bleak, *Annals*, April 30, June 3, 1869; "Manuscript Histories of the Church."

20. Hafner, *100 Years on the Muddy*, 46.

21. Andrew Jensen, comp., "History of the Muddy Valley Mission, 1847–1875"; reminiscences of Samuel Claridge, Church of Jesus Christ of Latter-day Saints Archives.

22. Elizabeth Wood Kane, *Twelve Mormon Homes*, 117.

23. Townley, *Conquered Provinces*, 47, 54.

24. *San Francisco Chronicle*, October 1, 1867, as quoted in M. Smith, "Lower Colorado River," 356; Young to Wm. H. Dame, Wm. F. Warren, and Hy. Lunt, March 2, 1865, and Young to Erastus Snow, March 2, 1865, Young letterpress copybook, Box 8, Folder 3.

25. Horatio, "Letter from Nevada," *Deseret News*, May 27, 1868; Townley, *Conquered Provinces*, 25.

26. Young to W. H. Hooper, February 4, 1868, Young letterpress copybook, Box 10, Folder 5.

27. Bleak, *Annals*, April 26, 1865, March 6, 1866; "Manuscript Histories of the Church."

28. Bleak, *Annals*, December 21, 1870.

29. Euzell Prince Preston, "The Prince Family in St. Thomas"; Hafner, *100 Years on the Muddy*, 52, 68–69; R. Cannon, "Aunt Hannah Sharp."

30. Hafner, *100 Years on the Muddy*, 74.

31. Helen Bay Gibbons, *Saint and Savage*, 127; Hafner, *100 Years on the Muddy*, 74.

32. Hannah Sharp, as quoted in L. A. Fleming, "The Settlements on the Muddy, 1865 to 1871: 'A God Forsaken Place,'" 157; Hafner; *100 Years on the Muddy*, 169; Thomas Day, *Journals and Letters of Elder Thomas Day*; Ellsworth, *Mormon Settlement on the Muddy*, 8.

33. George Washington Bean Papers, 3.

34. Bleak, *Annals*, April 21, 1865; "Manuscript Histories of the Church."

35. Joseph W. Young, "A Visit to the Muddy," *Deseret News*, June 19, 1868; Juanita Brooks, *On the Mormon Frontier: The Diary of Hosea Stout*, 461.

36. *Journal of Darius Salem Clement*; Corbett, "History of the Muddy Mission," 128.

37. Hafner, *100 Years on the Muddy*, 36.

38. Journal of Warren Foote, 196–97, as cited in Corbett, "History of the Muddy Mission," 122.

39. Bleak, *Annals*, February 18, 1866; "Manuscript Histories of the Church"; Reeve, *Making Space on the Western Frontier*, 105; Fleming, "Settlements on the Muddy," 159.

40. Journal of Price Nelson, 7, as cited in Corbett, "History of the Muddy Mission," 124; *Journal History* (April 2, 1866); R. Cannon, "Aunt Hannah Sharp."

41. Knack, *Boundaries Between*, 53.

42. Corbett, "History of the Muddy Mission," 125; Bleak, *Annals*, June 4, 1866.

43. Bleak, *Annals*, June 4, 12, 1866.

44. Kanosh was a member of the church and one of the earliest Native Americans to participate in temple ordinances, receiving his "endowment." Young to Thomas S. Smith, August 15, 1866, Young letterpress copybook, Box 9, Folder 4.

45. Delaun Mills Cox, "History of Delaun Mills Cox: Written by His Daughters with His Help and Approval in His 80th Year, Supplemented by His Diary, Originals Secured from Mrs. Susie Wilson, Hurricane, Utah," 11–12.

46. Young to Snow, January 2, 1868, Young letterpress copybook, Box 10, Folder 4; Hafner, *100 Years on the Muddy*, 74; *Journal of Darius Salem Clement*; Young to Jesse C. Little, December 25, 1868, Young letterpress copybook, Box 11, Folder 3; "Manuscript Histories of the Church."

47. J. Young, "Visit to the Muddy"; Monique Kimball, "A Matter of Faith: A Study of the Muddy Mission," 106; R. Cannon, "Aunt Hannah Sharp."

48. R. Cannon, "Aunt Hannah Sharp"; Mary Amelia Richards Streeper letters.

49. J. Young, "Visit to the Muddy."

50. *Journal of Darius Salem Clement*; Reeve, *Making Space on the Western Frontier*, 53–54; R. N. Fenton to E. S. Parker, February 14, July 12, 1870, Letters Received by the Office of Indian Affairs, 1824–1881, Nevada Superintendency, 1861–80, 1870–1871, UNLV Microforms, E 93 U95x Reel 539.

51. Bleak, *Annals*, April 26, 1865.

52. Young to Brigham Young Jr., October 18, 1865, Young letterpress copybook, Box 8, Folder 5; Bleak, *Annals*, December 31, 1865; *Journal History* (November 13, 1865).

53. Bleak, *Annals*, August 29, 1865.

54. Journal of Warren Foote, 187–88, as cited in Corbett, "History of the Muddy Mission," 96.

55. Darius S. Clement, "1868," as quoted in Kimball, "Matter of Faith," 46.

56. Bleak, *Annals*, June 3, 6, 1869; *Journal of Darius Salem Clement*.

57. Bleak, *Annals*, August 5, 1869; *Journal of Darius Salem Clement*.

58. McClintock, *Mormon Settlements in Arizona*, 120.

59. Wood, "William Wood." This was directly from his journal, which was published by the Daughters of the Utah Pioneers.

60. Bleak, *Annals*, January 20, May 1867; Young to Snow, January 2, 1868, Young letterpress copybook, Box 10, Folder 4.

61. Young to A. Carrington, Young letterpress copybook, Box 22, Folder 4; Bleak, *Annals*, June 3, 1869; "Manuscript Histories of the Church."

62. Bleak, *Annals*, June 3, August 5, 1869.

63. Corbett, "History of the Muddy Mission," 55; Don Ashbaugh, "Ghost Towns of Nevada: St. Thomas, Part 2," *Las Vegas Review-Journal*, April 10, 1960.

64. Bleak, *Annals*, December 1, 1870.

65. Hafner, *100 Years on the Muddy*, 55–56.

66. Ibid., 68–69, 292; R. Cannon, "Aunt Hannah Sharp"; Erastus Snow, quoted in *Journal of Discourses*, edited by G. Cannon, April 8, 1868, 12:214–15.

67. Cox, "History of Delaun Mills Cox," 13–14.

68. Betsy Jane Tenney Loose Simons diary, February–March 1866, as quoted in Audrey M. Godfrey, "Colonizing the Muddy River Valley: A New Perspective," 125; "Manuscript Histories of the Church." Snow was referencing the popular pioneer hymn "Put Your Shoulder to the Wheel."

69. Bleak, *Annals*, January 20, 1867.

70. Ibid., December 16, 1867; Hafner, *100 Years on the Muddy*, 50; Jensen, "History of the Muddy Valley Mission." Quoted in Ellsworth, *Mormon Settlement on the Muddy*.

3 · *Now That We Are Here, Where Are We? Boundary Disputes and the Abandoning of St. Thomas*

1. Hafner, *100 Years on the Muddy*, 71.

2. Ogden, Salt Lake City, and Provo all lay at the base of the Wasatch Mountains. The entire urban corridor is often referred to by locals as the Wasatch Front. Southern Utah residents refer to their area as Dixie. The original LDS settlers to the area coined the term in the 1850s in reference to its being a cotton-producing area.

3. "Manuscript Histories of the Church."

4. Bleak, *Annals*, August 7, 1865; Thomas S. Smith to Erastus Snow, August 6, 1865, St. George Temple Archives, St. George, UT. Quoted in Corbett, "History of the Muddy Mission," 136.

5. Bleak, *Annals*, August 7, September 5, 1865; Townley, *Conquered Provinces*, 3.

6. Jane Percy Kowalewski, "Strange Bedfellows: Mormon and Miners in Southern Nevada," 65–68.

7. Reeve, *Making Space on the Western Frontier*, 46.

8. McClintock, *Mormon Settlements in Arizona*, 124–25; *Journal of Darius Salem Clement*.

9. The act reads: "An ACT providing for the organization of Rio Virgin County, and defining the boundaries thereof. Sec 1—Be it enacted by the governor and legislative Assembly of the Territory of Utah: That all that portion of Washington County, beginning where the east line of the State of Nevada intersects the 37th parallel of north lat., running thence north along the east line of the State of Nevada to a point due west of the summit of Clover Valley mountain, thence east to said summit to its

intersection with the gulch, (known as Beaver Dam Wash) thence down said wash to its junction with the Rio Virgin, thence due south to the 37th parallel, thence west along said 37th parallel to the place of beginning, shall be known and designated as Rio Virgin County. Sec. 2—The County Court of said county shall locate the county seat, and report to the Legislative Assembly. Sec. 3—Said Rio Virgin County is hereby attached to the Second Judicial District, and for representation in the Legislative Assembly shall be associated with Washington and Kane Counties until otherwise provided by law. Sec. 4—This Act shall be in force from and after its passage. Approved February 18, 1869." *Acts, Resolutions, and Memorials, Passed and Adopted by the Legislative Assembly of the Territory of Utah,* 18th sess., 1869, chap. 10, p. 7; "Manuscript Histories of the Church."

10. *Journal of Darius Salem Clement.* Saints use the term *apostate* to describe someone who has left the church and fights against it. Nevada Surveyor General Report of January 14, 1871, 16, as quoted in Corbett, "History of the Muddy Mission," 149.

11. Andrew Jensen, "History of the St. George Stake," January 1870, as quoted in Gillies, "History of Lincoln County," 48; Ellsworth, *Mormon Settlement on the Muddy,* 15; PAM 22691, Utah State Historical Society, Salt Lake City. The source is silent as to the name of the prosecuting attorney, but it is possible that it was Carlow, who had already served in an official capacity for Lincoln County in the past. Another possibility is E. W. Wandell, who was the district attorney for Lincoln County at the time. A reorganite is a member of the Reorganized Church of Jesus Christ of Latter-day Saints, now the Community of Christ. Though the two churches have diverged further in the past century and a half, initially the biggest difference is that members of the reorganized church believed that the rightful successor to Joseph Smith was his son Joseph Smith III, not Brigham Young.

12. Bleak, *Annals,* February 6, 1870.

13. "The Muddy Mission," Moapa Stake Records, June 6, 1870.

14. Corbett, "History of the Muddy Mission," 146; "Manuscript Histories of the Church." George A. Smith is not to be confused with George Albert Smith, who was the eighth president of the Church of Jesus Christ of Latter-day Saints. George A. was George Albert's grandfather and namesake. He was also a cousin to Joseph Smith Jr. St. George, Utah, was named after him.

15. "Manuscript Histories of the Church."

16. Hafner, *100 Years on the Muddy,* 75.

17. Bleak, *Annals,* December 14, 1870.

18. Moapa Stake Records. Of the sixty-three, forty-seven were men and sixteen women. Census information in Bleak, *Annals,* December 31, 1870.

19. Diary of Warren Foote, 210, as cited in Corbett, "History of the Muddy Mission," 157.

20. Disfellowshipping is a form of church discipline just under excommunication. A disfellowshipped member is forbidden to speak or offer prayers in meetings or hold a calling. Members who have been to the temple are generally stripped of their temple recommend as well. After completing the steps outlined by the disciplinary council that disfellowshipped the member, they can then be restored to full fellowship.

21. Ellsworth, *Samuel Claridge*, 108; Moapa Stake Records.

22. H. S. Eldridge was one of the seven presidents of the Seventy. The Seventy are traveling ministers directly under the authority of the apostles. Daniel Wells was an apostle and councillor to President Young in the First Presidency of the church. Daniel H. Wells to H. S. Eldridge, January 24, 1871, Young letterpress copybook, Box 12, Folder 4; *History of the Kanab Stake*, as quoted in Larson, "Agricultural Pioneering," 225–26. To ensure that President Young's wishes were followed, the bishops distributed the following for landowners to sign: "Know all men by these presents: That we the undersigned, do, for and in consideration of the good will which we have for our brethren who are broken up on the Muddy, and are seeking homes elsewhere, relinquish all our claims to land, houses and other improvements formerly owned by us in Long, or Berry, Valley. And we do hereby give our full, free, and unqualified consent for the brethren from the Muddy to take and occupy our claims in said Long, or Berry, Valley; the same to be set off to individuals, as their Bishops may deem best. And we do further covenant and agree, that we will never demand pay of these brethren for our claims and improvements in the aforesaid valley. As witness our hands this _____ day of _____ 1871." Bleak, *Annals*, circa January 19, 1871.

23. Ellsworth, *Samuel Claridge*, 110; Hafner, *100 Years on the Muddy*, 44.

24. Eugene H. Perkins, transcript of the Centennial Celebration by former residents of St. Thomas, January 8, 1965, Special Collections, University of Nevada, Las Vegas.

25. Young to H. S. Eldridge, March 7, 1871, Young letterpress copybook, Box 12, Folder 5; Ellsworth, *Samuel Claridge*, 109; Bleak, *Annals*, February 28, 1871.

26. Kowalewski, "Strange Bedfellows," 11.

4 · "Not a Town of the Past . . .": From Zion to the Silver State

1. Hafner, *100 Years on the Muddy*, 144.

2. Ellsworth, *Samuel Claridge*, 113.

3. Ivan J. Barrett, "History of the Cotton Mission and Cotton Culture in Utah," 159.

4. Young to Eldridge, March 7, 1861, Young letterpress copybook, Box 12, Folder 5.

5. According to Bleak's *Annals* (March 1, 1871), only 7 of the 150 settlers called to strengthen the Muddy Mission in the 1867 October General Conference were among those who settled in Glendale.

6. Wood, "William Wood."

7. "The Muddy Settlements," *Salt Lake Tribune*, September 21, 1873, 3.

8. *Deseret News*, January 26, 1875; "Manuscript Histories of the Church." This assertion is unsubstantiated by other sources. See Ellsworth, *Samuel Claridge*, 109.

9. Scott Gold, "It's a Historic Drought," *Los Angeles Times*, October 16, 2004, A1; Jori Provas, "The Death of a Town Called St. Thomas," *Las Vegas Sun*, October 5, 1969, 12. St. Thomas was not necessarily isolated from civilization, but it was a significant distance from the county seat of Pioche and the sheriff located there. See Florence Lee Jones, "St. Thomas Ends Second Cycle as Lake Floods Town," *Las Vegas Review-Journal*, June 18, 1938, 1:1–8; Dustin George, "Tales of the Old West," *Nevadan*,

September 6, 1970, 27; and James G. Scrugham, *Nevada: A Narrative of a Frontier Land*, as quoted in Gillies, "History of Lincoln County," 40, as quoted in "Manuscript Histories of the Church."

10. Eugene H. Perkins, *A Pioneer Family's Legacy*, 10. In E. Perkins, transcript of the Centennial Celebration (see chap. 3, n. 24), the man is identified as Jack Reed. This story may be apocryphal, but I included it because it appeared in various forms in several different sources.

11. I. C. U., "Muddy Valley," *Pioche Weekly Record*, October 14, 1882, 2:3.

12. Sally Zanjani, *Jack Longstreet: Last of the Desert Frontiersmen*, 12–16.

13. I. C. U., "Affairs at the Muddy," *Pioche Weekly Record*, September 16, 1882, 3:4; I. C. U., "Muddy Valley."

14. Zanjani, *Jack Longstreet*, 24; Tramp, "From the Muddy," *Pioche Weekly Record*, March 3, 1883, 3:4.

15. "Local Intelligence," *Pioche Weekly Record*, May 17, 1884, 3:1; December 25, 1886, 3:2; November 20, 1886, 3:1. "Megarrigle" may be James Ross Megarrigle, who moved from St. Thomas to Las Vegas in 1889 to work as a schoolteacher on the Stewart Ranch.

16. Interview with Andrew Sproul Jr., June 19, 1956, as quoted in Laraine Graf, "They Came, They Saw, and Then They Went Elsewhere."

17. Hafner, *100 Years on the Muddy*, 74.

18. R. N. Fenton to Ely S. Parker, January 2, 1871, Letters Received by the Office of Indian Affairs, 1824–1881, Nevada Superintendancy 1861–80, 1870–1871, UNLV Microforms E 93 U95X Reel 539.

19. N. Douglas, September 1870, ibid.

20. Henry A. Fish to Ely S. Parker, June 3, 1871, ibid.

21. Charles F. Powell to H. R. Clum, September 6, 1871, ibid.

22. Hafner, *100 Years on the Muddy*, 12; G. W. Ingalls to F. A. Walker, November 1, 1872, Letters Received by the Office of Indian Affairs, 1824–1881, Nevada Superintendancy 1861–80, 1872–1873, UNLV Microforms E 93 U95X Reel 540; letter from Acting Secretary of the Interior, Relative to the Condition of the Pi-Ute Indians, 42nd Cong., 3rd sess., 1873, House Ex. Doc. No. 66, serial set 1565, 2–3, as quoted in Reeve, *Making Space on the Western Frontier*, 54.

23. "Pioche Notes," *Deseret News*, June 18, 1873.

24. Daniel Bonelli to Francis A. Walker, August 8, 1872, Letters Received by the Office of Indian Affairs, 1824–1881, Nevada Superintendancy 1861–80, 1872–1873, UNLV Microforms E 93 U95X Reel 540.

25. "Torch-Bearing Redskins Feared; Indians Were Only Hunting Rabbits," *Las Vegas Review-Journal*, June 28, 1964.

26. Bleak, *Annals*, August 28, 1871.

27. *Pioche Daily Record*, April 16, 1873; Reeve, *Making Space on the Western Frontier*, 55–58; Daniel Bonelli to Edward P. Smith, December 3, 1873, Letters Received by the Office of Indian Affairs, 1824–1881, Nevada Superintendancy 1861–80, 1872–1873, UNLV Microforms E 93 U95X Reel 540.

28. Daniel Bonelli to Edward P. Smith, September 10, 1874, Letters Received by the Office of Indian Affairs, 1824–1881, Nevada Superintendancy 1861–80, 1874–1875, UNLV Microforms E 93 U95X Reel 541.

29. A. F. Barnes to Edward P. Smith, December 20, 1874, ibid.; *Pioche Daily Record,* April 16, 1873; Reeve, *Making Space on the Western Frontier,* 55–58.

30. Robert Logan to N. B. Booth, August 8, 1877, Letters Received by the Office of Indian Affairs, 1824–1881, Nevada Superintendancy 1861–80, 1876–1877, UNLV Microforms E 93 U95X Reel 542. One resident, Charles Byers, complained to the commissioner that the Paiute stole between one thousand and fifteen hundred dollars' worth of grain a year from his fields. Charles P. Byers to Bureau of Indian Affairs Commissioner, May 25, 1880, Letters Received by the Office of Indian Affairs, 1824–1881, Nevada Superintendancy 1861–80, 1880, UNLV Microforms E 93 U95X Reel 545. See also Blow Fly, "From the Lower End," *Pioche Weekly Record,* August 16, 1884, 3:3; and Zanjani, *Jack Longstreet,* 34–38.

31. David F. Myrick, ed., *Reproduction of Thompson and West's History of Nevada, 1881, with Illustrations and Biographical Sketches of Its Prominent Men and Pioneers,* 491, as quoted in M. Smith, "Lower Colorado River," 105. The information apparently came from Daniel Bonelli. See Reeve, *Making Space on the Western Frontier,* 77; and E. Perkins, *A Pioneer Family's Legacy,* 20.

32. George E. Perkins, *Old St. Thomas,* 2, as quoted in Larson, "Agricultural Pioneering," 217.

33. *Deseret News,* February 19, 1873, as quoted in M. Smith, "Lower Colorado River," 314; "Manuscript Histories of the Church."

34. State of Arizona, "Excerpts from Report of Irrigation Investigations in Utah by U.S. Department of Agriculture, Office of Experiment Stations, Bulletin No. 124," *Complainant v. State of California,* Palo Verde Irrigation District, Imperial Irrigation District, Coachella Valley County Water District, the Metropolitan Water District of Southern California, City of Los Angeles, City of San Diego, and County of San Diego, Defendants, United States of America and State of Nevada, Intervenors, State of New Mexico and State of Utah, Parties. The Supreme Court of the United States, October 1956, no. 10 original, 253–55; Hafner, *100 Years on the Muddy,* 41.

35. Gillies, "History of Lincoln County, Nevada," 88–90; *Deseret News,* February 21, 1872; Sidney Whitmore, "The Papers of Sidney Whitmore"; Dorothy Dawn Frehner Thurston, *A River and a Road,* 53.

36. Hafner, *100 Years on the Muddy,* 96.

37. Larson, "Agricultural Pioneering," 216; "Papers of Sidney Whitmore"; E. Perkins, *A Pioneer Family's Legacy,* 11–12; G. Perkins, *Old St. Thomas,* 2, as quoted in Larson, "Agricultural Pioneering," 217; *Deseret News,* January 26, 1875; Hafner, *100 Years on the Muddy,* 180. Population numbers are unavailable for the 1890 census. Those census records were destroyed in a fire in the basement of the Commerce Building in Washington, DC, in March 1896. Tramp, "From the Muddy."

38. I. C. U., "Muddy Valley."

39. E. Perkins, *A Pioneer Family's Legacy*, 11–12; Bleak, *Annals*, October 18, 1885, March 3, 1891.

40. Kowalewski, "Strange Bedfellows," 11.

41. Hafner, *100 Years on the Muddy*, 183, 292. Mr. McGargle may be James Ross Megarrigle, who was a schoolteacher.

42. John Whipple, "The Coffeepot Rescue and the Six-Shooter Fire," 10.

43. Bleak, *Annals*, December 31, 1899.

44. The town of Kingman was founded in 1883 along the route of the Santa Fe Railroad and was a regional supply depot. Hafner, *100 Years on the Muddy*, 158.

45. State of Arizona, "Excerpts from Report of Irrigation Investigations," 251, 243–54.

46. Jesse P. Holt Jr., "Defends the 'Muddy,'" *Deseret News*, June 20, 1896; Andrew Jensen, "The Muddy Valley," *Deseret News*, March 23, 1892.

5 · *The Mountains Brought Down and the Valleys Exalted*

1. A. E. Cahlan, "From Where I Sit," *Las Vegas Sun*, September 19, 1966, 8:7–8.

2. US Census 10, 12, 13, 14, 15 data for St. Thomas, Nevada.

3. Hafner, *100 Years on the Muddy*, 98; "Moapa Valley," *Las Vegas Age*, May 16, 1908, 6.

4. "Talks About Clark County," *Las Vegas Age*, September 18, 1915, 1; "St. Thomas," *Las Vegas Age*, July 30, 1910, 1; US Department of Agriculture—Soil Conservation Service, Clark County, Nevada, Conservation District, and Nevada Division of Water Resources, *Flood Hazard Analyses, Las Vegas Wash and Tributaries, Clark County, Nevada: Special Report, History of Flooding, Clark County, Nevada, 1905–1975*, 6–8, 10–11.

5. Hafner, *100 Years on the Muddy*, 98; Vivian Frehner, *Memories of Matilda Reber Frehner*, 5.

6. "The Nevada Gold Butte Mines Co.—Ltd.," *Salt Lake Mining Review*, December 30, 1905; "Growing Interest in Gold Butte," *Salt Lake Mining Review*, February 15, 1906.

7. "St. Thomas to the Front," *Salt Lake Mining Review*, August 15, 1906.

8. "Growing Interest in Gold Butte"; "Mining Enterprise," *Las Vegas Age*, June 10, 1910, 1.

9. "New 'Dream' Borax Mine Bought by 'Borax' Smith," *Salt Lake Mining News*, March 30, 1921.

10. "Growing," *Las Vegas Age*, May 4, 1907.

11. Hafner, *100 Years on the Muddy*, 102.

12. Dennis McBride, "The Mormon Atlantis," 85.

13. "Harry Gentry Passes Away," *Washington County*, June 9, 1921; Hafner, *100 Years on the Muddy*, 102.

14. Andrew Jensen, Church Chronology, September 18, 1908; interview with Doris Reber, as quoted in Graf, "They Came, They Saw."

15. Hafner, *100 Years on the Muddy*, 127.

16. Everett Syphus, "Everett Syphus History."

17. Inez Gibson Waymire, "Robert O. and Edith H. Gibson"; Hafner, *100 Years on the Muddy*, 113.

18. Hafner, *100 Years on the Muddy,* 9.

19. Ibid.; Preston, "Prince Family."

20. Interview with Reber, as quoted in Graf, "They Came, They Saw"; Preston, "Prince Family"; Hafner, *100 Years on the Muddy,* 116.

21. McBride, "The Mormon Atlantis," 84.

22. A. D. Hopkins, "Wagon Freight Business Made Anything Else Look Easy," *Las Vegas Review-Journal,* May 12, 2005, AA17; Thurston, *River and a Road,* 56.

23. J. Young, "Visit to the Muddy" (see chap. 2, n. 35).

24. "Railroad News," *Las Vegas Age,* February 1, 1908.

25. "St. Thomas," *Las Vegas Age,* April 25, 1908, 4; "Moapa Valley—Railroad Down Muddy Valley Soon to St. Thomas," *Las Vegas Age,* May 9, 1908, 5.

26. "St. Thomas"; "Moapa Valley," *Las Vegas Age,* October 23, 1909, 5.

27. "Valley Improves," *Las Vegas Age,* April 29, 1911, 1.

28. Ibid.; "Railroad to St. Thomas," *Salt Lake Mining Review,* May 15, 1911.

29. "Fruit Festival," *Las Vegas Age,* June 10, 1911, 1; "St. Thomas Has Railroad," *Las Vegas Age,* March 16, 1912, 1; "Branch Opened," *Las Vegas Age,* May 4, 1912, 4. During this two-month period, there was almost a daily update on the progress of the construction.

30. "Moapa Mining Notes," *Las Vegas Age,* September 23, 1911, 4.

31. The story contains no clues as to what makes a hammer handsome. "Popular Lady to Drive Spike," *Las Vegas Age,* May 25, 1912, 1; Hafner, *100 Years on the Muddy,* 219.

32. "Special Train for Excursion," *Las Vegas Age,* June 1, 1912, 1.

33. "New Stake Organized," *Washington County,* June 13, 1912; Jensen, "Church Chronology," June 9, 1912.

34. "Terminal Town," *Las Vegas Review-Journal,* March 8, 1913, 1; Hafner, *100 Years on the Muddy,* 111; San Pedro, Los Angeles, and Salt Lake Railroad, *The Arrowhead;* interview with Reber, as quoted in Graf, "They Came, They Saw."

35. "Mountain of Salt," *Las Vegas Age,* May 30, 1908; "St. Thomas Salt Mine Lease Deal Is Closed," *Las Vegas Age,* January 9, 1926; "Shipping Much Salt from St. Thomas Mine," *Las Vegas Age,* February 2, 1918, 4; "Talks About Clark County."

36. Thurston, *River and a Road,* 56; "Cactus Kate Is in Wonderland," *Los Angeles Times,* May 16, 1916, 3:4.

37. "Big Improvements," *Las Vegas Age,* June 7, 1913; "New Railway Through Vegas," *Las Vegas Age,* June 6, 1913, 1; "Gold Near Moapa," *Las Vegas Age,* October 15, 1915, 1:6; "Another Railroad?," *Las Vegas Age,* June 2, 1917, 1.

38. "Have Good Lands; Want Good Roads," *Washington County,* April 10, 1913; "Virgin Valley Boosts Road," *Las Vegas Age,* April 5, 1913; "Government Will Survey Road," *Las Vegas Age,* July 4, 1914, 1.

39. Hafner, *100 Years on the Muddy,* 146, 160.

40. "Automobile Road Located," *Las Vegas Age,* August 23, 1913, 1; "Virgin Valley Favors Roads," *Las Vegas Age,* November 8, 1913, 1; "Meeting at Moapa," *Las Vegas Age,* March 28, 1914, 2.

41. "Auto Highway to Be Opened," *Las Vegas Age*, May 1, 1915, 1; "Normal Boys Build Roads," *Los Angeles Times*, November 26, 1916, 6:8.

42. "Auto Excursion to St. Thomas," *Las Vegas Age*, May 15, 1915, 1.

43. "St. Thomas Gives Royal Welcome," *Las Vegas Age*, June 6, 1915, 1.

44. "'Cactus Kate' Name for Car," *Los Angeles Times*, April 18, 1915, 7:1; "Cactus Kate Is in Wonderland"; "Cactus Kate Is in Salt Lake," *Los Angeles Times*, May 22, 1916, 1:6. The sandstone was not the only natural landscape feature that was a tourist draw. The salt mines were also an attraction. "Arrowhead Trail, a Common Sense Road Through a Land of Rare Beauty and Romance, Leads from Los Angeles to Salt Lake," *Los Angeles Times*, May 28, 1916, 6:15. Residents were the road crews at the time.

45. "Arrowhead Trail, a Common Sense Road"; C. H. Biglow, "Something About the Arrowhead Trail," *Washington County*, November 23, 1916.

46. J. F. Gibbs, "The Wilds of South Nevada," *Richfield Reaper*, March 15, 1906.

47. *Las Vegas Sun* editor A. E. Cahlan said that the opposite was true. He wrote, "'The Valleys' were a political power in those days and, because they voted together with only a few mavericks, they regularly decided elections—not only county but state. Politicians were quite aware of this fact and spent several million dollars over the years building two bridges over the Virgin River so that Bunkerville would be on the highway." Cahlan, "From Where I Sit." US Department of Agriculture—Soil Conservation Service, Clark County, Nevada, Conservation District, and Nevada Division of Water Resources, *Flood Hazard Analyses*, 11.

48. "County Road Funds in Splendid Shape," *Las Vegas Age*, August 11, 1917, 1; "Road Day Planned for the Arrowhead Trail," *Las Vegas Age*, February 23, 1918, 1.

49. Provas, "Death of a Town" (see chap. 4, n. 9).

6 · *Not with a Bang, but a Whimper*

1. "Bridge Opened on Arrowhead Trail," *Washington County*, March 24, 1921; US Department of Agriculture—Soil Conservation Service, Clark County, Nevada, Conservation District, and Nevada Division of Water Resources, *Flood Hazard Analyses*, 14.

2. H. L. Baldwin, *Preliminary Report of the Survey of the Proposed Boulder Canyon Reservoir and Dam Site on the Colorado River in Nevada and Arizona* (Department of the Interior, Reclamation Service, February–June 1919), 3, 8–9, 13–14, 16–17; "Arizona Exhibit no. 45: Problems of Imperial Valley and Vicinity," S. Doc. No. 142, 67th Cong., 2nd sess., 1922, a.k.a. "Fall-Davis Report," Arizona vs. California: 24 California Exhibits, vol. 24, miscellaneous, NARA, Denver, CO.

3. Baldwin, "Preliminary Report," 9–10.

4. McBride, "The Mormon Atlantis," 87; "Reservoirs for Colorado River," *Salt Lake Mining Review*, August 15, 1919; "U.S. Reclamation Service Begins Work," *Las Vegas Age*, November 19, 1921, 1.

5. Hafner, *100 Years on the Muddy*, 114.

6. "First State Corn Show," *Washington County*, December 13, 1923.

7. Hafner, *100 Years on the Muddy*, 111.

8. W. W. Johnston, *Classification of Privately Owned Lands—Boulder Canyon Reservoir—Boulder Canyon Project* (Department of the Interior, Reclamation Service, March 18, 1931), 1; Waymire, "Robert O. and Edith H. Gibson."

9. US Department of Agriculture—Soil Conservation Service, Clark County, Nevada, Conservation District, and Nevada Division of Water Resources, *Flood Hazard Analyses*, 13, 32; Hafner, *100 Years on the Muddy*, 75.

10. "Governor Describes Nevada's Buried City," *Las Vegas Age*, December 6, 1924, 1; Leslie Higginbotham, "Lost City Discovered in Nevada Sands," *New York Times*, 20:4; Harrington, "Primitive Pueblo City," 262.

11. "Pueblo Theory Substantiated," *Los Angeles Times*, March 23, 1923, A3; Al Parmenter, "Indian Gone from City Thousands of Years," *Los Angeles Times*, December 7, 1930, E1; "Archeology in the U.S.A.: Very Ancient Ruins Found in Nevada," *Times* (London), March 13, 1925, 13.

12. Hafner, *100 Years on the Muddy*, 358.

13. Dick Arnold, "St. Thomas Celebrates on July Fourth," *Las Vegas Age*, July 9, 1921, 1.

14. "Definite Plans for Highway Construction," *Las Vegas Age*, February 11, 1922, 5.

15. "Reports on Route for Arrowhead Trail," *Las Vegas Age*, November 8, 1919, 1, 6; Hafner, *100 Years on the Muddy*, 121; Ashbaugh, "Ghost Towns of Nevada" (see chap. 2, n. 63).

16. "Favor Changes in Route of Highway," *Las Vegas Age*, March 4, 1922, 1.

17. "Arrowhead Trail in Good Condition Says Lecturer," *Washington County*, March 9, 1922; "Sierra Summit Not Open Yet," *Las Vegas Age*, May 6, 1922; Provas, "Death of a Town" (see chap. 4, n. 9); Hafner, *100 Years on the Muddy*, 53.

18. "St. Thomas Gains in Population," *Las Vegas Review-Journal*, April 26, 1930, 1:4.

19. Hafner, *100 Years on the Muddy*, 229–30; Senator Tasker Oddie to Ray Lyman Wilbur, secretary of the interior, September 19, 1930, Bureau of Reclamation Collection, NARA.

20. Harry E. Crain to Elwood Mead, December 15, 1930, Bureau of Reclamation Collection, NARA.

21. Mead to Crain, December 18, 1930, and Mead to W. W. Johnson, December 23, 1930, ibid.; Johnston, "Classification of Privately Owned Lands," 3.

22. W. B. Acker, comptroller general of the United States, to the secretary of the interior, March 27, 1931, Bureau of Reclamation Collection, NARA. This boilerplate was extracted from USDOI-GLO acting commissioner to Stanley Summeril, August 16, 1931, ibid.

23. Levi Syphus to Crain and Cecil W. Creel, April 13, 1931, ibid., 15.

24. Oddie to Curtis D. Wilbur, secretary of the interior, August 22, 1931, ibid. One cannot help but wonder if the effectiveness of this letter was blunted by an error in addressing it. The letter is directed to Curtis D. Wilbur, secretary of the interior. Curtis Wilbur was a judge for the Ninth Circuit Court of Appeals in San Francisco and brother to Ray Lyman Wilbur, who was the secretary of the interior.

25. J. H. Alexander to Richard J. Coffey, March 2, 1931, ibid.

26. Mead to Chief Engineer [Walker Young], August 26, 1931, ibid.

27. Walker R. Young and J. R. Alexander, *Appraisal of Lands Which Will Be Flooded by Hoover Reservoir—Boulder Canyon Project* (Department of the Interior, Bureau of Reclamation, October 7, 1931), 11.

28. "St. Thomas Ranchers Receive Average of $2000 for Holdings to Be Flooded," *Las Vegas Review-Journal*, November 28, 1931, 1:7; "Ranch Owners Get Offers for Lands, Water," *Garfield County*, December 11, 1931; "Nearly Third of Million Paid Out for Land to Be Inundated," *Las Vegas Review-Journal*, August 4, 1932, 3:1–3.

29. Clark, Richards, and Bowen to Judge Dent, April 4, 1932, Bureau of Reclamation Collection, NARA.

30. Richard Lyman to Mead, October 11, 1932, ibid.

31. W. Young to Mead, November 4, 1932, ibid.

32. Ibid.

33. Lyman to Mead, Bureau of Reclamation Collection, NARA (emphasis added).

34. As quoted in McBride, "The Mormon Atlantis," 89.

35. Young and Alexander, *Appraisal of Lands*, 4.

36. W. Young and J. R. Alexander to Mead, December 2, 1931, Bureau of Reclamation Collection, NARA.

37. Mead to Oddie, April 14, 1932, ibid.

38. Mead to Lyman, November 1, 1932, ibid.

39. McBride, "The Mormon Atlantis," 89.

40. Jones, "St. Thomas Ends Second Cycle" (see chap. 4, n. 9).

41. "Mormon Church May Buy Ranch in Nevada," *Garfield County*, 24 June 1932.

42. "Clark County Ranchers May Lead in Colonization of Pahrump Area," *Las Vegas Review-Journal*, April 6, 1932, 1:4–5; "Mormon Town May Be Moved to New Place," *Denver Post*, April 23, 1932; "Removing a Town," *Las Vegas Review-Journal*, April 23, 1932, 8:1–2.

43. Harry Crain to Mead, 25 April 1932, Bureau of Reclamation Collection, NARA.

44. Frehner, *Memories of Matilda Reber Frehner*, 7.

45. Lyman to Mead, Bureau of Reclamation Collection, NARA.

46. T. S. Eliot, "The Hollow Men," in *Selected Poems*.

7 · *Coup de Grace?*

1. Provas, "Death of a Town" (see chap. 4, n. 9).

2. Saint Thomas Ward Moapa Stake General Minutes, 1910–1933.

3. Elton Garrett, "Last St. Thomas Pioneers Graves Moved to Escape Waters of Lake," *Boulder City Journal*, March 4, 1935, 2; Dustin George, "Tales of the Old West," *Nevadan*, September 6, 1970, 27.

4. "Moving Graves to Start Soon," *Las Vegas Review-Journal*, December 20, 1934, 1:7; Garrett, "Last St. Thomas Pioneers Graves Moved."

5. "Waters of Lake Near St. Thomas," *Las Vegas Review-Journal*, July 3, 1935, 1:1; "St. Thomas Will Miss Flood Another Year," *Las Vegas Evening Review-Journal*, May 27, 1936, 1:3; "Moapa Valley Notes," *Las Vegas Review-Journal*, March 1, 1937, 6:3.

6. Kathy Atchley, "Death of St. Thomas."

7. "St. Thomas Will Be Completely Submerged Within Next 2 Days," *Las Vegas Evening Review-Journal*, June 8, 1938, 1:6–7.

8. Cahlan, "From Where I Sit" (see chap. 5, n. 1); "Hugh Lord to Make Dam Lake Force Him from His Dwelling," *Las Vegas Review-Journal*, June 9, 1938, 1:3–4; "Hugh Lord, St. Thomas Pioneer, Finally Deserts Ground to Lake," *Las Vegas Review-Journal*, June 6, 1938, 1:3–4.

9. Hafner, *100 Years on the Muddy*, 53; Atchley, "Death of St. Thomas"; "Two Lone Dogs Keep Vigil at St. Thomas as Lake Waters Rise," *Las Vegas Review-Journal*, June 13, 1938, 1:3–4.

10. A Cover Fan [H. D. Sterling?], "St. Thomas, Nevada, Last Day Cancellation," *Western Stamp Collector*, July 16, 1938, 7:1–3.

11. Florence Lee Jones, "Last Resident Deserts Home Saturday Night to Lake Water," *Las Vegas Review-Journal*, June 13, 1938, 1:2; Atchley, "Death of St. Thomas."

12. William E. Warne to chief engineer, date unknown, Bureau of Reclamation, NARA. In the dateline on the letter, it reads "25" and contains a notation that the letter was sent with the improper date. There is a bureau date stamp of October 8, 1943, but it was clearly written before another letter on the same topic dated August 21, 1943.

13. District counsel Coffey to commissioner, August 21, 1943, ibid. In the Tucker Act (1887), the US government waived its sovereign immunity from lawsuits.

14. W. Young to commissioner, August 27, 1943, ibid.

15. Bureau of Reclamation acting regional director to commissioner, April 16, 1945, ibid.

8 · *Sodden Phoenix*

1. "St. Thomas Up from Watery Grave," *Las Vegas Review-Journal*, April 10, 1945; William S. Riley, "Remember St. Thomas? Here 'Tis Again, Back from Depths of Mead," *Las Vegas Review-Journal*, May 23, 1945, 10:1–8.

2. Ed Oncken, "'Ghost' City of St. Thomas Not to Emerge from Lake Mead This Year," *Las Vegas Review-Journal*, circa 1948; "Ordinance, So Help Me, Protects St. Thomas Beasts," *Las Vegas Review-Journal*, February 21, 1951, 3:6–7.

3. Interview with Everett Syphus, St. George, November 20, 1974, as quoted in Graf, "They Came, They Saw"; "Old Ghost City of St. Thomas Is Back," *Las Vegas Review-Journal*, March 23, 1953.

4. "Ghost Town Pilgrimage: A Visit to St. Thomas," *Las Vegas Review-Journal*, December 30, 1964.

5. E. Perkins, transcript of the Centennial Celebration (see chap. 3, n. 24).

6. Berkeley L. Bunker, transcript of the Centennial Celebration by former residents of St. Thomas, January 8, 1965, Special Collections, University of Nevada, Las Vegas.

7. John L. Smith, "Town's Ruins Emerge from Water to Whisper," *Las Vegas Review-Journal*, February 20, 2003, B1.

8. National Park Service, "Director's Order #75A: Civic Engagement and Public Involvement," http://www.nps.gov/policy/DOrders/75A.htm.

9. J. Smith, "Town's Ruins Emerge from Water to Whisper."

10. Darrell Wade, "Letter to the Editor," *Las Vegas Review-Journal,* July 5, 2004, B6.

11. Henry Brean, "Agency Hopes to Protect Sites," *Las Vegas Review-Journal,* November 12, 2005, B2; Scott Gold, "It's a Historic Drought," *Los Angeles Times,* October 16, 2004, A1.

12. Liz Ševcenko and Maggie Russell-Ciardi, "Sites of Conscience: Opening Historic Sites for Civic Dialogue," 10, 13.

13. Ken Ritter, "An 'Atlantis' Rises from the Desert," *Los Angeles Times,* August 31, 2003, B1.

14. J. Smith, "Town's Ruins Emerge from Water to Whisper." The issue was also discussed in Gold, "It's a Historic Drought"; and Phoebe Sweet, "Lake's Ghost Town Seen as a Warning," *Las Vegas Sun,* March 12, 2008.

Bibliography

Archival Resources

Acts, Resolutions, and Memorials, Passed and Adopted by the Legislative Assembly of the Territory of Utah. Utah State Historical Society Archives, Salt Lake City.

Atchley, Kathy. "Death of St. Thomas." Nevada Day Program, October 31, 1962. St. Thomas Folder. Las Vegas City Library Vertical Stacks.

Bean, George Washington. Papers. MSS 1038. L. Tom Perry Special Collections, Harold B. Lee Library, Brigham Young University, Provo, UT.

Bleak, James Godson. *Annals of the Southern Utah Mission.* Church of Jesus Christ of Latter-day Saint Archives, Salt Lake City, UT.

Brigham Young University. Provo, UT.

Bunker, Berkeley L. Transcript of the Centennial Celebration by former residents of St. Thomas, January 8, 1965.

Bureau of Reclamation Records. Bureau of Reclamation Collection. National Archives and Records Administration, Denver, CO.

Church of Jesus Christ of Latter-day Saint Archives. Salt Lake City, UT.

Clement, Darius S. "1868." Diary, papers, account books, and notebooks. Church of Jesus Christ of Latter-day Saints Archives, Salt Lake City, UT.

———. *Journal of Darius Salem Clement.* Church of Jesus Christ of Latter-day Saints Archives, Salt Lake City, UT.

Cox, Delaun Mills. "History of Delaun Mills Cox: Written by His Daughters with His Help and Approval in His 80th Year, Supplemented by His Diary, Originals Secured from Mrs. Susie Wilson, Hurricane, Utah." Utah State Historical Society, Salt Lake City.

Day, Thomas. *Journals and Letters of Elder Thomas Day.* M270.1D2744d1978. Church of Jesus Christ of Latter-day Saints Archives, Salt Lake City, UT.

Ellsworth, S. George. *Mormon Settlement on the Muddy.* Dello G. Dayton Memorial Lecture. Ogden: Weber State College Press, 1985.

Frehner, Vivian. *Memories of Matilda Reber Frehner.* Special Collections, University of Nevada, Las Vegas.

Ipson Family Papers. MSS SC 627, Brigham Young University Special Collections. Provo, Utah.

Jensen, Andrew. "Church Chronology." Church of Jesus Christ of Latter-day Saints Archives, Salt Lake City, UT.

———, comp. "History of the Muddy Valley Mission, 1847–1875." Church of Jesus Christ of Latter-day Saints Archives, Salt Lake City, UT.

———. *History of the St. George Stake.* Church of Jesus Christ of Latter-day Saints Archives, Salt Lake City, UT.

Journal History of the Church of Jesus Christ of Latter-day Saints. Church of Jesus Christ of Latter-day Saints Archives, Salt Lake City, UT.

Las Vegas City Library, Las Vegas, NV.

"Manuscript Histories of the Church: The Muddy Mission." MS 4029, Roll 8. Church of Jesus Christ of Latter-day Saints Archives, Salt Lake City, UT.

Moapa Stake Records. Church of Jesus Christ of Latter-day Saints Archives, Salt Lake City.

"Mrs. Elizabeth Claridge McCune." MSSA 1593. Utah State Historical Society, Salt Lake City.

National Archives and Records Administration. Denver, CO.

Preston, Euzell Prince. "The Prince Family in St. Thomas." In *Memories.* Special Collections, University of Nevada, Las Vegas.

Saint Thomas Ward Moapa Stake General Minutes, 1910–1933. CR 7798 11. Church of Jesus Christ of Latter-day Saints Archives, Salt Lake City, UT.

San Pedro, Los Angeles, and Salt Lake Railroad. *The Arrowhead.* Utah State Historical Society, Salt Lake City.

Streeper, Mary Amelia Richards. Letters, 1849–68. MS 9340. Church of Jesus Christ of Latter-day Saints Archives, Salt Lake City, UT.

Syphus, Everett. "Everett Syphus History." In *Memories.* Special Collections, University of Nevada, Las Vegas.

University of Nevada, Las Vegas.

Utah State Historical Society. Salt Lake City, UT.

Waymire, Inez Gibson. "Robert O. and Edith H. Gibson." In *Memories.* Special Collections, University of Nevada, Las Vegas.

Whitmore, Sidney. "The Papers of Sidney Whitmore." MSS 48. Special Collections, University of Nevada, Las Vegas.

Wood, James H. "William Wood on the Muddy Valley Mission, 1867–72."

Young, Brigham. Letterpress copybook, MS 2736. Church of Jesus Christ of Latter-day Saints Archives, Salt Lake City, UT.

Newspapers

Boulder City Journal (Nevada)
Cloudburst (Las Vegas)
Denver Post
Deseret Evening News
Deseret News
Garfield County (Utah)
Las Vegas Age
Las Vegas Review-Journal
Las Vegas Sun
Los Angeles Times
Millard County Chronicle (Utah)

Nevadan
New York Times
Pioche Weekly Record (Nevada)
Richfield Reaper (Utah)
Salt Lake Mining News
Salt Lake Mining Review
Salt Lake Tribune
San Francisco Chronicle
Times (London)
Tonopah Daily Sun (Nevada)
Washington County (St. George, UT)
Western Stamp Collector (Oregon)

Other Sources

Arrington, Leonard J., Feramorz Y. Fox, and Dean L. May. *Building the City of God: Community and Cooperation Among the Mormons.* Urbana: University of Illinois Press, 1976.

Baldwin, Edward E. "Las Vegas in Popular Culture." PhD diss., University of Nevada, Las Vegas, 1997.

Barnett, Tim P., and David W. Pierce. "When Will Lake Mead Go Dry?" *Water Resources Research* 44 (March 2008).

Barrett, Ivan J. "History of the Cotton Mission and Cotton Culture in Utah." Master's thesis, Brigham Young University, 1947.

Brimhall, George W. *The Workers of Utah.* Provo, UT: Inquirer, 1889.

Brooks, Juanita. *On the Mormon Frontier: The Diary of Hosea Stout.* Vol. 2. Salt Lake City: University of Utah Press, 1964.

Cannon, George Q., ed. *Journal of Discourses.* 26 vols. Liverpool: F. D. Richards, 1886.

Cannon, Ramona Wilcox. "Aunt Hannah Sharp and the Muddy Mission." *Relief Society Magazine* (October 1926).

Corbett, Starr Pearson. "A History of the Muddy Mission." Master's thesis, Brigham Young University, 1968.

Darrah, William Culp. "George Y. Bradley's Journal, May 24–August 30, 1869." *Utah Historical Quarterly* 15 (1947).

Dellenbaugh, Frederick S. *A Canyon Voyage.* New York: G. P. Putnam's Sons, 1908.

The Doctrine and Covenants of the Church of Jesus Christ of Latter-day Saints. Salt Lake: Corporation of the President of the Church of Jesus Christ of Latter-day Saints, 1981.

Eliot, T. S. *Selected Poems.* New York: Harcourt, Brace, and World, 1964.

Ellsworth, S. George. *Samuel Claridge: Pioneering the Outposts of Zion.* Logan, UT: self-published, 1987.

Euler, Robert C. *Southern Paiute Ethnohistory.* Salt Lake City: University of Utah Press, 1966.

Fleming, L. A. "The Settlements on the Muddy, 1865 to 1871: 'A God Forsaken Place.'" *Utah Historical Quarterly* 35 (Spring 1967).

Frémont, John Charles. *Report of the Exploring Expedition to the Rocky Mountains in the Year 1842, and to Oregon and California in the Years 1843-44.* Chicago: Bilford Clark, 1887.

Garreau, Joel. *The Nine Nations of North America.* Boston: Houghton Mifflin, 1981.

Gibbons, Helen Bay. *Saint and Savage.* Salt Lake City, UT: Deseret Book, 1865.

Gillies, Richard E. "A History of Lincoln County, Nevada, 1776-1874." Master's thesis, University of Utah, 1959.

Godfrey, Audrey M. "Colonizing the Muddy River Valley: A New Perspective." *Journal of Mormon History* 22, no. 2 (1996).

Graf, Laraine. "They Came, They Saw, and Then They Went Elsewhere." Paper, Dixie College, 1974.

Hafen, Leroy R., and Ann W. Hafen. *Journals of Forty-Niners: Salt Lake to Los Angeles.* Lincoln: University of Nebraska Press, 1998.

———. *The Old Spanish Trail.* Glendale, CA: Arthur H. Clark, 1954.

Hafner, Arabell Lee. *100 Years on the Muddy.* Springville, UT: Art City, 1967.

Harrington, Michael R. "A Primitive Pueblo City in Nevada." *American Anthropologist,* n.s., 29, no. 3 (1927).

Harrison, Clifford Dale. *The Ashley-Smith Explorations.* Cleveland, OH: Arthur H. Clark, 1918.

Jackson, Richard H. "The Mormon Village: Genesis and Antecedents of the City of Zion Plan." *BYU Studies* 17 (Summer 1975).

Jensen, Andrew, ed. "History of the Las Vegas Mission." *Nevada State Historical Society Papers, 1925-1926.* Reno: Nevada State Historical Society, 1926.

Kane, Elizabeth Wood. *Twelve Mormon Homes.* Salt Lake City, UT: Signature, 1972.

Kelly, Isabel T. *Southern Paiute Ethnography.* Salt Lake City: University of Utah Press, 1965.

Kimball, Monique. "A Matter of Faith: A Study of the Muddy Mission." Master's thesis, University of Nevada, Las Vegas, 1988.

Knack, Martha. *Boundaries Between: The Southern Paiute, 1775-1995.* Lincoln: University of Nebraska Press, 2004.

Kowalewski, Jane Percy. "Strange Bedfellows: Mormon and Miners in Southern Nevada." Master's thesis, University of Nevada, Las Vegas, 1984.

Larson, Andrew Karl. "Agricultural Pioneering in the Virgin River Basin." Master's thesis, Brigham Young University, 1946.

McBride, Dennis. "The Mormon Atlantis." *Nevada* (November-December 1993).

McClintock, James H. *Mormon Settlements in Arizona.* Phoenix, AZ: self-published, 1921.

Meinig, D. W. "The Mormon Culture Region: Strategies and Patterns in the Geography of the American West, 1847-1964." *Annals of the Association of American Geographers* 55 (June 1965).

Myrick, David F., ed. *Reproduction of Thompson and West's History of Nevada, 1881, with Illustrations and Biographical Sketches of Its Prominent Men and Pioneers.* Berkeley, CA: Howell-North, 1958.

Nash, Gerald. *The American West Transformed: The Impact of the Second World War.* Lincoln: University of Nebraska Press, 1990.

Nelson, Lowry. *The Mormon Village: A Pattern and Technique of Land Settlement.* Salt Lake City: University of Utah Press, 1952.

Nevins, Allan. *Fremont, the West's Greatest Adventurer.* New York: Harper and Brothers, 1928.

Peirce, Neil R. *The Mountain States of America: People, Politics, and Power in the Eight Rocky Mountain States.* New York: W. W. Norton, 1972.

Perkins, Eugene H. *A Pioneer Family's Legacy.* The Ute Vorace Perkins Family Organization of Moapa Valley, Nevada. Provo, UT: privately published, 2002.

Powell, John W. *The Exploration of the Colorado River and Its Canyons.* New York: Dover, 1961.

Reeve, W. Paul. *Making Space on the Western Frontier: Mormons, Miners, and Southern Paiutes.* Urbana: University of Illinois Press, 2007.

——. "Mormons, Miners, and Southern Paiutes: Making Space on the Nineteenth-Century Western Frontier." PhD diss., University of Utah, 2002.

Reps, John. *Cities of the American West: A History of Frontier Urban Planning.* Princeton, NJ: Princeton University Press, 1979.

Rothman, Hal. *Neon Metropolis: How Las Vegas Shed Its Stigma and Became the First City of the Twenty-First Century.* New York: Routledge, 2003.

Scrugham, James G. *Nevada: A Narrative of a Frontier Land.* Vol. 1. Chicago: American Historical Society, 1935.

Ševcenko, Liz, and Maggie Russell-Ciardi. "Sites of Conscience: Opening Historic Sites for Civic Dialogue." *Public Historian* 30, no. 1 (2008).

Smith, Joseph, Jr. *History of the Church of Jesus Christ of Latter-day Saints.* Edited by B. H. Roberts. 7 vols. Salt Lake City, UT: Deseret News Press, 1902–32.

Smith, Melvin T. "The Lower Colorado River: Its History in the Lower Canyons Area." PhD diss., Brigham Young University, 1972.

Stegner, Wallace. *Mormon Country.* Lincoln: University of Nebraska Press, 1970.

Szasz, Ferenc Morton. *Religion in the Modern American West.* Tucson: University of Arizona Press, 2002.

Thurston, Dorothy Dawn Frehner. *A River and a Road.* Mesquite, NV: self-published, 1994.

Townley, John M. *Conquered Provinces: Nevada Moves Southeast, 1864–1871.* Provo, UT: Brigham Young University Press, 1973.

US Department of Agriculture—Soil Conservation Service, Clark County, Nevada, Conservation District, and Nevada Division of Water Resources. *Flood Hazard Analyses, Las Vegas Wash and Tributaries, Clark County, Nevada: Special Report, History of Flooding, Clark County, Nevada, 1905–1975.* August 1977. Reno: US Department of Agriculture, Soil Conservation Service, 1977, prepared in cooperation with the Nevada Division of Water Resources and local organizations.

Walker, Ronald W. "Golden Memories: Remembering Life in a Mormon Village." *BYU Studies* 37 (1997–98).

Whipple, John. "The Coffeepot Rescue and the Six-Shooter Fire." *Beehive History* 26 (2000).

Winnemucca, Sarah. *Life Among the Paiutes: Their Wrongs and Claims*. Bishop, CA: Chalfant Press, 1883.

Zanjani, Sally. *Jack Longstreet: Last of the Desert Frontiersmen*. Reno: University of Nevada Press, 1988.

Index

rodent infestations, 85
Ronnow, C. C., 93
Rufus (Paiute chief), 39

Salt Lake railroad, 86
salt mining, 47, 71–72, 87, 89, 90
Sandwich Islanders, 13–14
San Pedro, Los Angeles & Salt Lake Railroad, 87, 88, 91
Saunders, Leslie R., 117, 118–19
schools, 48, 73–74
Scrugham, James, 82, 99, 100
Sellers, William, 81
Sharp, Hannah, 20, 23, 34, 41, 48
silver mining, 17, 71
Simons, Betsy, 48–49
Smith, Charles Pears, 34
Smith, Edward, 69
Smith, Francis "Borax," 81
Smith, George A., 15, 27, 55–57
Smith, George Albert, 83
Smith, Jedediah Strong, 10, 12
Smith, John L., 1, 122–23
Smith, Joseph: on the importance of forming communities, 26; the plat concept and, 24–25
Smith, Melvin T., 18
Smith, Thomas Sassen: as acting bishop, 29; bishop of St. Thomas Ward, 51; blessing of St. Thomas's first child, 28; farming, 43; interactions with the Southern Paiute, 37; Nauvoo Legion, 39–40; settlement of St. Thomas and, 2, 19, 22–23, 33; state boundary disputes involving St. Thomas, 51
Smoot, Reed, 105
Snow, Erastus: communication between Mormon settlements and, 30; cotton production in the Muddy Mission and, 61; interactions with the Moapa Paiute, 35–36, 39–40, 41; irrigation canal proposal, 44; Mormon abandonment of St. Thomas and, 56–57, 58; Mormon policy toward mining and, 17; Nauvoo Legion, 39–40; Nevada's attempts to tax St. Thomas and, 54–55; settlement of the Muddy River Mission and, 27, 28;

site location for St. Thomas, 33; on St. Thomas residents who wintered in the north, 49
soft-shelled-almond production, 71
Southern Pacific Railroad, 32–33, 112
Southern Paiutes: concept of reciprocity and conflicts with Americans, 11–12; early descriptions and accounts of, 8–10; Indian agents and the Paiute reservation, 42–43; interactions with Mormons, 7, 13, 14, 15–16, 35–42; name for the Moapa Valley, 12; relationship with the Ute and Navajo, 13; settlement in the Moapa Valley, 8. *See also* Moapa Paiutes
Southern Utah Mission, 13, 16
Southwestern Pacific Railroad, 91
Southwest Nevada Indian Agency, 67–70
Sproul, Andrew, 65–66
St. George, 27, 30, 51, 58
St. Joseph, 53, 88
St. Joseph Branch, 27
St. Thomas: accounts and descriptions following the Mormon abandonment, 60, 63–66; accounts and descriptions from the early 1900s, 77–76; agriculture and irrigation (*see* agriculture; irrigation ditches/canals); climate and summer heat, 30–32, 94; communication with other Mormon settlements, 30; community and social life in the 1860s and 1870s, 48; community and social life in the 1920s, 100–101; community and social life in the early 1900s, 84–85; cotton production and economy, 46–47; death and submergence in Lake Mead, 2, 111–13, 114–17; dissatisfaction of Mormon residents, 48–49; early descriptions of, 34–35; early Native American inhabitants, 8–10; economic growth in the early 1900s, 79–82; emergences from Lake Mead, 1, 3, 120–21, 122; floods, 79, 96, 99, 101; geographic location, 2; Great Basin expeditions and, 29–30; growth in the 1880s and 1890s, 73–76; historical significance of, 2–4; Hoover Dam construction and (*see* Hoover

Dam construction); importance of the Mormon Church to, 22, 82–83; Indian agents and the Paiute Indian reservation, 66–70; interactions with the Paiutes following the Mormon exodus, 60, 65–66, 68–69, 70–71, 134n30; interactions with the Paiutes in the early 1900s, 83–84; Lost City ruins and, 8, 96, 99–100; Mormon abandonment of, 50, 56–59, 60–63, 132n22; Mormon presence in the early 1900s, 82–83; Mormon return to in 1880, 60, 72–73; Mormon settlement (*see* St. Thomas settlement); mosquitoes and malaria, 31; National Park Service adminsitration and the policy of civic engagment, 3, 5, 122–24; Nevada's attempts to tax, 52–53, 54–56, 59; Old Spanish Trail and, 10–11; population growth in the early 1900s, 78–79; railroads and, 32–33, 86–91; regional water usage issues and, 1, 5, 123–24; reunions of former residents, 121–22; road construction and improvements, 91–95 (*see also* Arrowhead Trail highway); schools, 73–74; state boundary disputes, 50–56; tourism and, 100, 101; treasure hunters and, 122–23; water sources and supply problems, 1, 2–3, 44, 46; water system and sewage disposal, 78; Brigham Young's 1870 visit to, 49
St. Thomas cemetery, 115
St. Thomas Loop, 123
St. Thomas Mining District, 71, 80
St. Thomas settlement: American settlement patterns of the West and, 22; arrival of the first Mormon settlers, 2, 6–7, 22–24; calls for Mormon missionaries and settlers between 1865 and 1869, 27–29; jurisdiction issues, 27; Mormon families in, 28; Mormon home construction, 33–34; Mormon inhabitation of poor lands and wilderness, 26–27; Mormon interactions with the Southern (Moapa) Paiutes, 7, 13, 14, 15–16, 35–42; Mormon settlement plans and, 22; Mormon town plat pattern, 24–26; reasons for Mormon settlement

in the Muddy River valley, 12–20; role of Brigham Young in, 4, 6, 13–20, 23, 25, 27, 28–29, 32, 35; site location, 33
St. Thomas Ward, 51, 60, 74, 82, 90, 114–15
Standard Oil, 86
Star Pony mail route, 73
state boundary disputes: the abandonment of St. Thomas and, 50, 56–59; states claiming St. Thomas, 2, 27, 50–56
Stegner, Wallace, 25
Sterling, H. D., 116–17
Stewart, Helen, 88
Stewart, Henry G., 67
summer heat, 30–32, 94
surveys and survey crews, 96–98, 104
Syphus, Clara, 81
Syphus, Edward, 72, 90
Syphus, Everett, 83
Syphus, June, 115
Syphus, Levi, 81, 90, 93, 102, 104–5, 106–9
Syphus, Luke and Julie, 60
Szasz, Ferenc Morton, 4

Tabuts, 8
taxation: Nevada and the taxation of St. Thomas, 52–53, 54–56, 59
Taylor, John, 72
telegraph lines, 30
"Terminal Town," 90
Ter-ra-Kuts, 69
the Seventy, 132n22
Thomas (Paiute chief), 37–38, 39
To-ish-obe, 35–36, 38, 39
Tolan, T. O., 90
tourism, 100, 101
Townley, John, 32
town plat pattern, 24–26
treasure hunters, 122–23
"treaties," 38
trucks, 91–92
Turner, Frederick Jackson, 3
Tut-se-gavits (Paiute chief), 39

Uintah Indian Reservation, 39
Union Pacific and Oregon Short Line railroad, 88
Union Pacific Railroad, 32–33, 87, 100